The Ultimate Mental Toughness Guide:

Roller Derby

Naomi "Sweetart" Weitz

Cover Design and Art by Skyler Weitz

ISBN: 0692330461
ISBN-13: 9780692330463

DEDICATION

This book is dedicated to roller derby. When I found roller derby, I found home. I am indebted.

CONTENTS

ACKNOWLEDGMENTS

Thank you to my two boys, Skyler and Asher, for sharing me with roller derby. Thank you to all of the amazing photographers: DreamTeam Photography, Cory Lund, TJ Chase, Brendan Zwelling, Christopher Chase, and Robert Massey. Thank you to the skaters whose interviews give this book its voice: Loogie Vuitton, Punching Judy, Wombpunch, EMTease, Pinktastic, Paisley, and OC Triple D.

1

WHAT IS MENTAL TOUGHNESS TRAINING?

You're in the last 15 minutes of the game and your team is down in points. How do you react? Do you give up? Do you decide that your team has lost when the game isn't over yet? Are you imagining how refreshing that beer will be at the afterparty? If so, those thoughts can actually cause you to lose. Your thoughts can manifest into reality.

Every skater makes a decision when they see that their team is losing and it is getting close to the end of the game. They choose to play harder or they choose to give up.

Have you ever noticed two teams can be neck and neck the entire game and at some point there is a momentum shift and one team will jump out ahead in points? What is happening here? When you eliminate problems with endurance or injuries what you have left is a breakdown in a team's mental game. Mental toughness has come into play.

So what is mental toughness? Mental toughness is using psychological principles to improve an athlete's performance. An athlete's performance is about 40% physical and 60% psychological. Some experts say mental toughness skills factor in even more! Mental toughness skills can be learned and when the skills are practiced they will not only improve your derby game, but also keep the sport you love fun. In fact, the skills that you will learn in this book can be applied to any performance setting, not just sports. Many business professionals, musicians, public speakers and more use mental toughness skills to maximize their success.

> *The mind and body can't be separated.*

Consider what would happen if someone were to ask you to walk across a board 6 inches wide, 20 feet long, and 10 inches above the ground. You would be able to do this without hesitation. However, if the board were 80 feet above the ground you might become paralyzed by the fear of falling. Even though there is no difference in the physical skill required, your mental state would inhibit your ability to complete this task and actually increase the chances that you would fail. Your attention would be focused on trying not to fall rather than on walking across the beam. This experiment illustrates the importance of mental toughness skills. In a high stakes situation where there is a lot on the line you can help yourself succeed by using psychological concepts to train the way you think, what you concentrate on, how relaxed you are and more.

Mental toughness training can help you do things like:

- Maximize motivation

- Deal with potential obstacles

- Create confidence

- Defeat self-doubts

- Increase focus

- Decrease anxiety

- Prevent burnout

Mental toughness helps athletes perform at their best by helping them gain control and consistency. With practice, an athlete will increase their awareness of the mental and physical states that allow them to play at their best. This awareness will help them regulate their bodies and minds. Mental toughness training should supplement your physical training in order for you to achieve your optimal derby performance.

Roller derby is currently dominated by women and this book is written to the adult, female participant. However, the concepts cross age and gender and are applicable to all roller derby participants. This book can be read in any order as each chapter deals with a separate aspect of mental toughness. So feel free to skip around and read the chapters in any order you want.

The core mental toughness skills can't be separated from each other. They overlap and are interwoven through all of the chapters so you can learn about them in different ways. This book attempts to give skaters as much performance enhancing information as possible. Varying points of

Copyright 2013, Cory Lund Photography

to affect the skaters who need to be going out there and kicking butt. You are a member of the team and the win (or loss) will belong to you as well.

Now that you have an idea of what mental toughness training is and how it can be applied let's dig in deeper!

Try this: Are You Mentally Tough?

Take this short mental toughness quiz to see where your skills are at today:

1. Before a game I
   a. Always set goals
   b. Sometimes set goals
   c. Never set goals

2. Whether I am winning or losing I
   a. Always believe in myself
   b. Believe in myself only when I'm winning
   c. Rarely believe in myself and think I'm a failure

3. Distractions during a game
   a. Don't bother me
   b. Sometimes bother me, but I can easily refocus
   c. Take my focus fully away from my performance

4. My emotions, thoughts and breathing in a game are usually
   a. Something I can control and use to my advantage
   b. Inconsistent, but are in my control when I am doing well
   c. Not in my control, my breathing is too fast and I have a hard time reacting

5. After a game, the self-evaluation of my performance is
   a. Normally accurate about what my strengths and weaknesses were that day
   b Not always accurate, but I can pick out some key things I need to improve
   c. Never accurate because I don't ever evaluate my performance

---

Answers

A's are worth 3 points each. B's are worth 2 points each.

C's are worth 0 points each.

12–15: You are very mentally tough.

8–11: You are somewhat mentally tough.

4–7: You could benefit from more mental toughness.

0–3: Uh oh, you need to learn some mental toughness skills.

The ideal psychological profile for a successful athlete includes the following characteristics:

- Highly self-confident

- Expects success

- Able to feel energized yet relaxed

- Feels in control

- Able to focus on the task at hand

- Sees difficult situations as exciting and challenging

- Has high standards but is flexible enough to learn from mistakes

- Has a positive attitude about performing

- Is determined and committed

This book will help you to become all these things and more. Regardless of your score on the quiz, keep on reading. Whether you are learning them for the first time or getting refreshers for things you already know, mental toughness skills will help you to be your best in roller derby and in life!

> *"I don't have the athlete's mentality, which I've been trying to get. I've noticed that athletes can just push themselves and push themselves. I don't like running. I've had to push myself so hard to get my ass up and go running. I think running is like the worst thing in the world."*
>
> *— Paisley, age 21, fresh meat*

2

BE SELF-AWARE

Self-awareness is the mental toughness skill that will set the foundation for you being able to learn all of the other skills. Self-awareness is the capacity to know where you are at emotionally, what drives you, and what your effect is on others. It is necessary to know where you're at in order to know where you want to go and how to get there. Self-awareness requires being honest with yourself. The most basic question that needs to be answered is, *Am I thinking and acting in a way that will allow me to skate at my best?* A highly self-aware person has the self-confidence to be truthful and realistic about their motivations, actions and abilities.

Being self-aware means knowing what you are thinking. What are you telling yourself in your head? Is it positive or negative? Do you blame others? What do you say to yourself when you make a mistake? Whose voice is it that you hear? Are you your own cheerleader? Do you put yourself down? Are you plagued by self-doubts? How do your actions affect others? How do your actions affect yourself? Being self-aware also means knowing what you are feeling and doing. This will set the stage for you to begin to understand how the three elements — thoughts, feelings and actions — are connected and what you can do to make necessary changes to break up unhelpful cycles.

Mindfulness

The core of Buddhist practice is *mindful* meditation. To be mindful is to approach all with wakefulness. Part of mindful practice is being aware, but not judgmental, of our emotions. When we are being mindful there are no bad feelings or good feelings, just feelings. If we feel an emotion we can simply notice it, and say to ourselves something like, *Oh that's interesting, I am feeling really angry right now.* We notice our feelings in a detached sort of way. By observing our emotions at a distance we gain the ability to be objective and decide how we want to react, if at all. Being mindful means we don't have to respond with either words or actions or unhelpful attitudes. We can merely observe our feelings like we would observe a cloud in the sky.

Mindfulness can also apply to our awareness of other aspects of our lives including our bodies and our surroundings. When we are mindful of our bodies we can have gratitude for all that they do for us. We can notice areas that may need some TLC so we can be as healthy as possible. We can gain a better technical performance because we will know where our different body parts are and what they are doing. When we are mindful of our surroundings we can appreciate the strengths of our team members and understand the big picture during games. This will allows us to use the best strategies possible.

Mindfulness is a skill that is closely related to self-awareness. When we are being mindful we are being the opposite of mindless. While this may seem like a big "duh", take a second to really think about this concept. Think about a mindless activity that you do. This could be a chore, exercise, driving, or anything else you can do without putting a lot of thought into it. You may even daydream while you are doing the activity. A mindless activity does not require your full attention. Being mindful, on the other hand, means you are paying full attention. You are fully aware of your thoughts, your feelings, your body and your environment. You are completely immersed in the activity and in the moment. In order to play your very best game you need to be mindful. The ability to be mindful helps you in your quest for self-awareness by increasing your ability to be focused on the present and allowing you to see yourself, others and your environment as less emotionally charged.

Try this: Mindfulness

Look through the pictures in a magazine. Pay attention to your emotional reactions. Do you feel angry? Do you think something is sad? Notice what you think about the pictures, but don't judge your thoughts or feelings as being bad or good. By observing your own observations you are creating distance between your emotions and your actions. This gives you the ability to choose how you act and you won't have to *react*.

The Zone

A concept related to being mindful is the *zone* or sometimes called the *flow state*. You may have heard athletes talk about being "in the zone" during a particularly successful game. What exactly is the zone? According to positive psychologist, Mihaly Csikszentmihalyi, who coined the term *flow*, this state of being is one of the most enjoyable and valuable that a person can have. According to Csikszentmihalyi, the flow state involves "being completely involved in an activity for its own sake. The ego falls away. Time flies. Every action, movement, and thought follows inevitably from the previous one, like playing jazz. Your whole being is involved, and you're using your skills to the utmost."

> *Freedom is where my skates are.*

The flow state feels both demanding and rewarding at the same time. Have you ever been so involved in something enjoyable that you lost track of how much time had passed? This could be playing music, creating something artistic, or any project that you became completely immersed in. Were you so involved in the activity that everything around you seemed to fade away? Did you lose yourself entirely to the activity? If so, that is what being in the zone feels like.

Csikszentmihalyi's model explains why some tasks are much easier than others. If you have ever been able to have this experience during a game, those were most likely the times when you played at your absolute best and had the most fun. You may have felt like you didn't have to think about what your body was doing — it was on autopilot. Your actions probably felt spontaneous and effortless. You may have heard the final whistle and felt amazed that the game was over.

This is what the being in the zone feels like:

- Being completely involved in what you are doing

- A sense of being outside everyday reality

- Great inner clarity

- Experiencing balance between your ability levels and the challenge

- Having a clear understanding of what you want to achieve

- Lacking awareness of bodily needs

- Knowing that you can do the task at hand

- Not worrying about yourself

- A sense of timelessness

- Feeling internally motivated

When you are in the zone you are skating with great focus, incredible confidence and presence in the moment. The zone has been thought of as this magical, mystical place where you're performing at your peak all the time. In reality, the athlete is constantly making adjustments to get their best performance. There are many things you can do to help your chances of getting into the zone. You can do this by learning mental toughness skills. You can focus on the right things at practice and at games. You can be completely absorbed in each moment you are skating. You can be confident in your skills, your teammates, your coaches, and your training. You can make sure not to let self-doubts and negativity get in the way of your success. Finally, when it's time for a game, don't hold back. Game time is not the time to play cautiously and controlled. It is the time to show what you can do!

The next time you are going into a game be mindful, but not judgmental, of your thoughts. Be aware of how confident you are that you have the skills to meet the task at hand. Do you feel anxious because you think your skills aren't where they need to be to meet the challenge? Or do you feel apathy because you feel the challenge isn't high enough for your skills? If you feel too anxious then it would be time to do a relaxation technique. If you feel apathetic then you can do an energizing technique to increase concentration and effort. You can learn how to adjust your energy level in Chapter 6.

To get into the zone, the skater must find a good match between their skills and the task at hand. The sweet spot is right between stressed out and boredom.

Ideally, a skater will feel confident in their skills and seek out high level challenges to meet them. These are the

16

conditions for getting into the zone. Once you've experienced it you can begin to learn what you can do to increase your chances of it happening more often. There are three conditions for the flow state:

1. **Goals:** You must be working towards a greater goal to experience the flow.

2. **Balance:** There must be a balance between where you think your skills are and how challenging you perceive the task at hand to be.

3. **Feedback:** You need to have immediate feedback on your performance so that you can make adjustments. This feedback can come from others or from your own self-awareness of how you are doing.

The All-Or-Nothing Syndrome

Sometimes athletes develop an all-or-nothing syndrome regarding their performance. They believe they either accomplished what they were trying to do or they didn't. Such as, a blocker may think she either knocked the jammer out of bounds or she didn't. Or a jammer might feel she either had a great jam or she didn't. All-or-nothing thinking can cause a skater to have an overly negative view of their performance. This type of thinking can hinder progress because it puts too much focus on end results and not enough on the steps that are needed to get you there. A coach can help a skater increase awareness of the gradations needed to begin to successfully execute a skill. Say a skater is learning hitting. All of the focus shouldn't be on whether or not the outcome was perfect. When learning a skill the skater should focus on all of the different pieces involved in the development of a skill. For example, the skater could work on increasing their awareness of how low they were. The coach could ask the skater to rate their lowness on a scale from 1 to 5 following each attempt. The number 5 would represent the ideal lowness necessary to execute a good solid hit. Using this method, the skater could see that she was making progress learning effective hitting even though she didn't knock anyone down or out. Here are some examples of all-or-nothing thinking and more helpful ways to think about your performance:

All-or-nothing thinking: *I didn't score any points.*

Helpful thinking: *I was able to take some good hits without getting knocked down. Now I need to work on my agility.*

All-or-nothing thinking: *I didn't knock her out of bounds.*

Helpful thinking: *My form was correct. If I increase my speed I will be more effective.*

With increased awareness, athletes can make more accurate corrections in their performance. Even though the outcome may not be perfect, you can maintain motivation during practices by seeing that at least part of your effort is successful.

Being Present

How often are you truly present or immersed in your game? Can you think of a game where you couldn't wait for it to end? Can you think of a game where you couldn't believe it was already over? Those two situations illustrate the difference between being present in the moment and being somewhere else.

If you aren't being present that means your head is either in the past or in the future. The past can be filled with all sorts of negative emotions including resentment, disappointment and anger. The future may be filled with negative thoughts including worry, doubt and fear. However, right NOW everything is fine. Right now is all that is real. You can handle right now. We can't change the past and we can't predict the future but we can be fully here *now*.

18

Try this: This Is It

Too often we are working towards ends in a game and not enjoying the means. We may be so engrossed in winning that we don't appreciate playing the game. Don't be in such a hurry to get somewhere else in time that you aren't enjoying where you're at.

It may be hard to believe if you are just embarking on your roller derby career, but even this most exciting and badass of sports can one day become a commonplace part of your life. One game may start to blend into the next. Practices, that at one time you couldn't wait for, may become tedious. Skaters may become jaded and forget to be grateful for this amazing opportunity. The reality is you probably won't be playing derby forever. It's an awesome moment in your life that you should savor. At your next game, slow down and take a moment to smell the derby roses. It may help to imagine that it is the very last game you'll ever play. Jon Kabat-Zinn, author of *Wherever You Go There You Are*, suggests "recognizing the bloom of the present moment" and affirming that "This is it."

Make a list of the moments you want to remember at your next game and then when they happen think to yourself, *This is it*. These are the reasons you do this. These are the reasons you love this. Appreciate every game like it's your last by focusing on the incredible moments that make derby what it is.

Some ideas are:

- Sitting next to your teammates on the bench waiting to go out for the next jam

- Making a sweet assist

- Doing your team cheer at the beginning of the game

- Having your name called by the announcer during introductions

- A little girl asking for an autograph

- Seeing the look on their jammer's face right before she gets hit

- That moment right before the first jam whistle of the game

- Lacing up your skates or strapping on your helmet

- High fiving your fellow skaters after some great teamwork

- Dancing on the jammer line with the opposing jammer

Try this: Where Are Your Skates?

Too often our head is not in the same place as our skates. When we are *present* our head and our skates are in the same place. You can use the question, "Where are my skates?" as a centering cue. This will help you to keep your thoughts only on the present and what is happening around you.

You can practice this at home so that when you get into a stressful game situation it will be easier to do:

1. Feel the floor underneath your feet. Feel the type of surface. Is it hard or lumpy? Soft or gritty? Focus in on the sensation of your feet connecting with the floor. Spend some time here getting grounded.

2. Use your senses to become engaged in what is around you. What do you see? What do you hear? What do you smell?

3. Keep your thoughts limited to the present moment and situation. If they drift away to anything outside of your immediate environment then gently bring them back.

Try this: Blind Skate

A great way to be completely immersed in the present moment is to skate "blind." This activity also works well as a trust-building exercise for teams.

1. Partner up with a teammate.

2. Set up some obstacles to maneuver around.

3. Blindfold yourself.

4. Have your teammate give you directions on when to turn, slow down, etc. in order to keep from tripping over the cones.

You will need to become hyperaware of elements you may not usually be super tuned in to such as your teammate's voice, the basic mechanics of skating and where your body is in space. You can also do this at home off-skates. Just close your eyes and try to slowly navigate around.

Try this: Self-Awareness Exercise 1

Sports psychologists, Robin S. Vealey and Christy A. Greenleaf, developed visualization exercises similar to the following to increase an athlete's sense of self-awareness. Try recording yourself or someone else reading the "scripts" and then play them back to yourself to practice this mental toughness skill.

Think back and choose a past derby performance in which you performed very well. Use all of your senses — hearing, touch, smell, sight and taste — to re-create that situation in your mind. See yourself as you were succeeding, hear the sounds involved, feel your body as you performed the movements, and re-experience the positive emotions. Try to pick out the characteristics that made you perform so well (intense focus, feelings of confidence, optimal energy levels). After identifying these characteristics, try to determine why they were present in this situation. Think about the things you did in preparation for this particular event. What are some things that may have caused this great performance?

Repeat this exercise, imagining a situation in which you performed very poorly. Make sure you are very relaxed before trying this because your mind will subconsciously resist your imagery attempts to re-create unpleasant thoughts, images and feelings. Attempt to become more self-aware of how you reacted to different stimuli (coaches, opponents, officials, fear of failure, needing approval from others) and how these thoughts and feelings may have interfered with your performance.

Try this: Self-Awareness Exercise 2

Think back to a derby situation in which you experienced a great deal of anxiety. Re-create that situation in your head, seeing and hearing yourself. Especially re-create the feeling of anxiety. Try to feel the physical responses of your body to the emotion and also try to recall the thoughts going through your mind that may have caused the anxiety. Now attempt to let go of the anxiety and relax your body. Breathe slowly and deeply and focus on your body as you exhale. Imagine all of the tension being pulled into your lungs and exhaled from your body. Continue breathing slowly and exhaling tension until you are deeply relaxed. Now repeat this exercise imagining a situation in which you experienced a great deal of anger, and then relax yourself using the breathing and exhalation technique.

Try this: Self-Awareness Exercise 3

The purpose of this exercise is to help you become more aware of the things that happen during competition that bother you when you perform. Think about times when your performance suddenly went from good to bad. Re-create several of these experiences in your mind. Try to pinpoint the specific factors that negatively influenced your performance (coaches, teammates, officials, opponents' remarks, opponents started to play much better). After becoming aware of the factors that negatively affected your performance, take several minutes to re-create the situations. Develop appropriate strategies to deal with the negative factors. Imagine the situations again, but this time imagine yourself using your strategies to keep the negative factors from interfering with your performance. Reinforce yourself by feeling proud and confident that you were able to control the negative factors and perform well.

Try this: Inventory Of Mental Toughness Skills

Taking an inventory of your mental toughness skills following practices and games can help you to pinpoint areas you did well in and areas in which you need to improve. A key component of being self-aware is honesty. It will not help you if you score yourself higher to save face or lower to appear modest. Keep inventories you completed after your best and worst performances so you can compare them. Over time you will be able to make your practices and games consistently positive.

> *Roller derby is an honest sport. Honesty with yourself and honesty with others is demanded.*

Inventory of Mental Toughness Skills

Name: _____ **Date:** _____

DIRECTIONS: Read each statement. Circle the best response:

I was focused

Agree   Somewhat Agree   Somewhat Disagree   Disagree

I was distracted

Agree   Somewhat Agree   Somewhat Disagree   Disagree

I was confident

Agree   Somewhat Agree   Somewhat Disagree   Disagree

I felt burned out

Agree   Somewhat Agree   Somewhat Disagree   Disagree

My self-talk was positive

Agree   Somewhat Agree   Somewhat Disagree   Disagree

I was anxious

Agree   Somewhat Agree   Somewhat Disagree   Disagree

It was hard for me to accept feedback

Agree   Somewhat Agree   Somewhat Disagree   Disagree

I was able to use imagery effectively

Agree   Somewhat Agree   Somewhat Disagree   Disagree

It was hard for me to deal with mistakes

Agree   Somewhat Agree   Somewhat Disagree   Disagree

I used goal setting

Agree   Somewhat Agree   Somewhat Disagree   Disagree

I put in 100%

Agree   Somewhat Agree   Somewhat Disagree   Disagree

I had a healthy competitive attitude

Agree   Somewhat Agree   Somewhat Disagree   Disagree

Inventory of Mental Toughness Skills

3

SET GOALS

This chapter covers the mental toughness skill of goal setting. The pursuit of goals is the basic regulator of human behavior. Without a destination or thoughts of "what comes next?" people would not move forward and would not be able to function at all. Even the most simple thought such as, "I'm going to put on my helmet now" can be thought of as a goal. Goals are necessary for the most basic of functioning but are especially necessary for meeting your potential in roller derby. Goals give skaters direction and focus for the work to be done.

The Merriam-Webster definition of a goal is "something that you are trying to do or achieve." Sports psychologists break down that definition into three different types of goals. *Outcome goals* focus on the results of a game such as beating someone. *Performance goals* focus on improvements relating to your own past performance such as increasing speed. *Process goals* focus on the specific techniques the skater uses such as transferring weight and following through when executing a hit. It is crucial for skaters to develop all three types of goals. Performance and process goals have been shown to be directly correlated to increased athlete performance. Setting only outcome goals can lead to dissatisfaction with the sport because there can only be one winner and if that is your only measure of success you are setting yourself up for a lot of disappointment.

> *"I left practice crying for the first 6 months. I took a long time to realize small progress is progress, that I wasn't going to be able to do 25/5 overnight, or do a successful hip check. I am still hard on myself with skills and laps."*
>
> *— Loogie Vuitton, age 32, skating 6 years.*

Set S.M.A.R.T.E.R. Goals

There are many different formats and methods for goal setting. However, there are some general guidelines that can be applied to all types of goal setting activities.

- Being able to set goals for where you want to go means having an honest and accurate awareness of where you are at right now.

- Be sure to set both short term and long term goals.

- Set positive goals as opposed to negative goals. That is, identify what it is you want to do, not what you don't want to do. For example, instead of jammers striving to stop back blocking, set a goal of slowing down, turning the body and aiming for legal target zones.

- Always evaluate your progress at least monthly and modify or change goals as needed.

- Don't forget to do *something* to work towards your goals every day.

An acronym that can help you with goal setting is S.M.A.R.T.E.R. This stands for Specific, Measurable, Action-oriented, Realistic, Timely, Evaluate and Re-evaluate.

Specific. Goals should be specific rather than vague or general. Instead of saying, "I want to be a better skater" try "I want to make the allstar team" or "I want to be able to skate one lap backwards in 20 seconds."

Measurable. There should be a way to measure your progress towards your goal or a way to know when you have achieved it. Be able to answer questions such as *How much? How many?* or *How will I know when I have accomplished my goal?* Including elements such as time or distance can help with that. You can also use another person such as a coach or a teammate as your measuring stick. For example, "My coach will tell me I am hitting with correct form."

Action-oriented. Goals need to be put into action. Many people think about goals and then stop there. Your goal needs to include elements that are about *doing*. If a goal is important for you to attain there should be something that you can do towards your goal every day. Becoming an amazing derby skater not only involves skating. Goals can incorporate non-skating actions such as improving diet, cross-training, quitting smoking, studying derby videos and so on.

Realistic. Your goal should be something that you are both willing and able to do. Making a good study of your past can help you gauge what you are capable of in the future. Goals should be moderately difficult so they pose a challenge, but realistic enough to be achieved. You must truly believe that your goal can be accomplished.

Timely. There needs to be an end time to your goal. When will you accomplish your goal by? Time frames tied to your goal give you a sense of urgency and can help to motivate you.

Evaluate and Re-evaluate. One of the biggest barriers to people accomplishing their goals is that they set goals and then never think about them again. There is also a misconception about goal setting that once goals are set they are final. This notion can be a huge obstacle for change. Take a look at your goals at least once per month. See how much progress you have made. It may be necessary to adjust your goals. You may be making improvements faster than you thought you would and may need to set new or more difficult goals. Or maybe some unforeseen obstacles have come up that necessitate making your goals easier or pushing out your timeline.

> *"I try to think of what I want to improve on and where I want to go with my league. I take a mental note of what I want to achieve and kind of set a deadline for myself."*
>
> *–EMTease, age 33, skating 5 years*

Set Practice Goals

It is important to not only set goals for games but for practice time. After all, this is where you are putting in the most hours. Practice goals can help to keep you motivated during long hours of repetitive or monotonous drills. An example of a practice goal is to work on aggression.

Don't forget to include character development or team building goals. You might say, *Tonight I am going to find something to laugh about with my teammate that I don't really get along with.* This is a preferable to *I will ignore her tonight* or *I am going to try to avoid getting grouped up with her for drills.* The first example is solution-oriented while the second two are problem-oriented, meaning they will perpetuate the issue rather than trying to fix it.

More examples of practice goals:

- I will pay attention when the coach is talking.

- I will volunteer first.

- I will try to be at the front of the pack.

- I will talk to one of the veteran skaters whom I feel shy around.

- I will try something I am afraid of.

- I will challenge myself by attacking the biggest threat, rather than the weakest link, during scrimmages.

- I will leave my bad day or personal issues at the door.

- I will ask one of the new skaters how their day was.

> *"I want to get around the track once before (the veteran skaters) get around it twice." –Paisley, age 21, fresh meat*

Will Power

One of the things that can get in the way of achieving your goals is lacking the determination and discipline needed to steadily work towards getting there. Often times obstacles will arise that can make a skater feel discouraged and want to give up. Imagine training for a year and then getting injured at the practice right before what was supposed to be your first game? Plan for ways to keep your resolve as you work towards your goals. This will help strengthen your will power in the face of difficulty.

Some ideas for reinforcing your commitment to your goals when you feel discouraged or frustrated:

- Get a friend involved to support and encourage you.

- Write out and memorize motivational phrases to tell yourself.

- Display inspirational photos where you can see them every day to remind you of your dreams.

In order to help you to succeed only set one or two goals to start out with. Once you gain experience in the process you can set more goals. Setting too many goals too soon can make you feel overwhelmed and lead you to abandon all of them.

Try this: What Is Your Dream Goal?

This method of goal setting is fun and different because you get to start with your dream goal and work backwards to more immediate, specific and tangible goals. It is a way to think of distant possibilities and then be able to transform your dreams into immediate actions. Complete the My Dream Goal worksheet and dream big!

My Dream Goal

1. My dream goal is: _____

_____

2. In one year I will: _____

_____

3. In six months I will: _____

_____

4. In one month I will: _____

_____

5. In one week I will: _____

_____

6. Tomorrow I will: _____

_____

Signature/Date: _____

Photo by TJ Chase

Try this: Goal Stepping

Goal stepping is a way to link short term goals to long term goals. The first step should be something you can achieve immediately but that will lead to more difficult and far reaching objectives. The example in Figure 3.1 shows the steps a skater could take if her goal was to jump over an obstacle one foot high. Notice the plan includes off-skates elements.

"I wanted to jam. I'm not a jammer by any means but just to try it and just get better endurance-wise. I went to more speed skating and did more trail skating. I started conditioning more and changed my diet and lifestyle."

— EMTease, age 33, skating 5 years

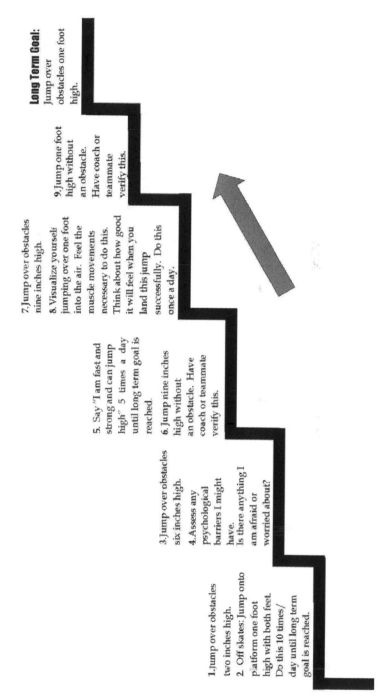

Long Term Goal: Jump over obstacles one foot high.

9. Jump one foot high without an obstacle. Have coach or teammate verify this.

7. Jump over obstacles nine inches high.

8. Visualize yourself jumping over one foot into the air. Feel the muscle movements necessary to do this. Think about how good it will feel when you land this jump successfully. Do this once a day.

5. Say "I am fast and strong and can jump high" 5 times a day until long term goal is reached.

6. Jump nine inches high without an obstacle. Have coach or teammate verify this.

3. Jump over obstacles six inches high.

4. Assess any psychological barriers I might have. Is there anything I am afraid or worried about?

1. Jump over obstacles two inches high.

2. Off skates: Jump onto platform one foot high with both feet. Do this 10 times/day until long term goal is reached.

Figure 3.1 Example of Goal Stepping

Try this: Mind Mapping

A mind map is an organic, visual tool that uses both sides of the brain in goal setting. When we use pictures, symbols or other images it involves the right side of our brain while words are the domain of the left side of the brain. A mind map is an artistic and creative way to clarify and focus the goals that are in your mind using colors, pictures and words. And like any good map, a mind map not only shows you where you want to go but how to get there.

There is no right or wrong way to make a mind map. Just start drawing and see where your mind leads you! Figure 3.2 shows an example of a mind map about the goal of balancing derby and personal life.

"I couldn't turn and do all the things I can now. I think that's pretty exciting." — Paisley, age 21, fresh meat

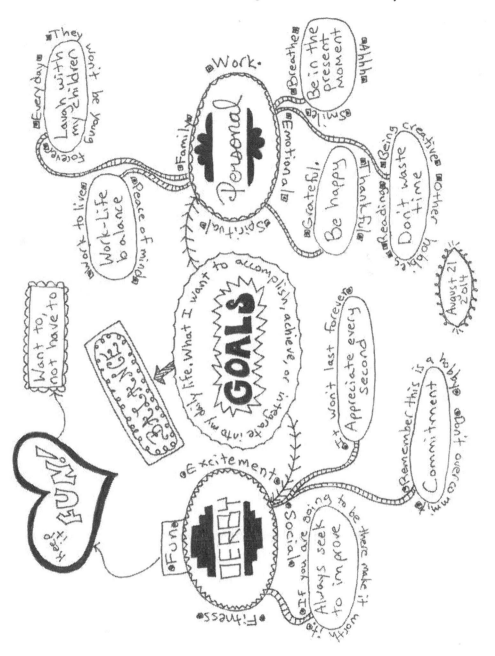

Figure 3.2 Example of a Mind Map

Establish A Pre-Game Routine

Your routine is like a funnel that will focus you in the right direction and on the right things. Your game routine can include everything from what meals you eat to the type of socks you wear to what music you listen to. Your routine will evolve over time. What is critical for you now may not be important in a year. Likewise, in a year you may not believe you played without some important aspect of your pre-game routine. Find what works for you, find what gets you ready to play your absolute best and try to make that happen as often as possible. Keep in mind that flexibility is also important. Don't put so much emphasis on your routine that you become unable to perform if an aspect is missing. Part of being an amazing athlete is being able to adapt to unexpected or undesirable situations and still be able to give 100%.

Sports psychologist Jennifer Etnier, in *Bring Your 'A' Game* (2009), writes that a good pre-game routine will warm up your body, help you to achieve the appropriate energy level and assist you to focus on the important aspects of the game. Etnier also suggests athletes develop a post-game routine to help them to deal with the emotions they may be experiencing following a competition. In the event of an upsetting loss it is important to take the time to take control of your feelings, focus on the positive aspects of your game and prepare to respond in a positive way to fans, friends, opposing team, family and teammates. The time to analyze your performance is when you have given yourself time to get your emotions settled down. This is mental toughness in action!

Establish a different pre-game routine for home and away games. Your away pre-game routine will include making sure you have everything you need packed so you don't have a duct tape emergency in a town where you don't know your way around. A pre-game routine for away games should start at least 48 hours ahead of the game. Your home pre-game routine should start at least 24 hours before game time.

Try this: Create A Pre-Game Routine

Create your own pre-game routine for both home and away games. Include meals, gear, uniform, music, mental and physical activities, warm ups and more. Be specific! In between competitions review your routine to see if there is anything you want to add, take away or adjust. Be sure to make it flexible as well so you don't completely freak out if you can't find your rainbow booty shorts! Figure 3.3 shows an example of a pre-game routine for a home game.

"I don't have a pair of socks or I don't have that pair of underwear to go bout in but I have a really good breakfast, a very solid good breakfast, and then I have a peanut butter and jelly sandwich about an hour before I bout. And I have sex with my husband before I bout. You're stretched out, you're warmed up and you feel kind of like a winner already. It's pretty easy. And the one time I didn't do it I broke my ankle. I'm not kidding. It gets me into my Judy. It gets me into my other persona." –Punching Judy, Age 47, skating 10 years

24 hours before game time Day/time: _____Fri/ 7 pm_____	Don't drink alcohol tonight! Healthy dinner with carbs- veggie lasagna. In bed by 11.
10 hours before game time Day/time: _____Sat/ 9 am_____	Game day! Go for a short run. Healthy breakfast, not too heavy- fresh juice and breakfast burrito. Hydrate!
6 hours before game time Day/time: _____Sat/ 1 pm_____	Light healthy lunch- spicy tuna roll and green tea. Get uniform ready. Hydrate!
2 hours before game time Day/time: _____Sat/ 5 pm_____	Have a nutritious snack- banana, energy bar, and pomegranate juice. This is the food that will be hitting me come game time.
1 hour before game time Day/time: _____Sat/ 6 pm_____	Listen to pre-game play list. Dynamic stretching. Get geared up. Briefly work muscles in all 3 planes. Do a few explosive starts. Warm up with team. Breathing- make sure expansive, not shallow. Body- scan and release any tension. Loosey goosey! Pee one last time. GO TIME BABY!
Post-game Day/time: _____Sat/ 9 pm_____	Static stretching. Think about what I/we did WELL. Drink H2O, have some beer and nachos at the afterparty!
Post-game Day/time: _____Sun/ 11 am_____	Sleep in! Long yoga session. Giant greasy breakfast and bloody Mary.

Figure 3.3 Example of a Pre-Game Routine

24 hours before game time

Day/time: _____

10 hours before game time

Day/time: _____

6 hours before game time

Day/time: _____

3 hours before game time

Day/time: _____

1 hour before game time

Day/time: _____

Post-game

Day/time: _____

Post-game

Day/time: _____

Figure 3.4 Pre-Game Routine Worksheet

"My pregame routine was heavily influenced by the veterans when I first started. What to eat, what not to eat, drink pedialyte, coconut milk, or energy drink. Now I eat lots of veggies and fruit on game day for hydration and nutrition! I don't have time to be picky! I drink lots of water the day before also. I need to take the hottest shower I can possibly stand, put on my stockings, skinz, and knee highs. Then sports bra, do my boutin' makeup and nails. Finally, the jersey!" — Loogie Vuitton, age 32, skating 6 years

Advance The Venue

Part of the nervousness stemming from travel games comes from being in an unfamiliar environment. Make advancing the venue part of your pre-game routine in order to reduce anxiety on game day. It is best if you have a chance to physically go check out the location where you will be playing. If you can go at the same time of day as when your game will be played you can get acclimated to the lighting. Bright lights can increase anxiety all by themselves and having to perform under bright lights when you are not used to them can make it even worse.

> *Having a plan of attack will build your self-confidence.*

Investigate as much as you can at the game venue. Where will the team benches be? Where are the restrooms? Where will your team be gearing up? If you can try out the skating surface do it! This is especially crucial if you are a newer skater and have not had the opportunity to get to know the differences between concrete, wood and skate court. Elite athletes and teams may even travel to a competition site days ahead of their event in order to acclimate to altitude and temperature.

If it is not possible to actually visit the game venue then do as much cyber research as you can. Find out where the game will be held and search for photos and videos of the location online. Check out the opposing team's website and see the faces of competition. See if you can find videos of them playing so you can see what their level of play is and what moves and strategies they

> *Never allow any negativity or self-doubts to enter your visualizations. Always image situations as you want them to be.*

are using. Then come game day it will feel like you've been there before! You can take all of that energy that would have been wasted on stress and put it into playing your best.

Try this: Use Imagery To Advance A Venue

You can use mental imagery to be able to enter a variety of real situations, including game venues, with a comfortable feeling of familiarity. Make your mental images as realistic and detailed as possible. Use as many of your senses as you can: sights, sounds, smells, tastes and touch.

Get comfortable and close your eyes. Imagine you are driving into the venue parking lot. What time of day is it? Who is with you? What are you thinking and feeling? See and feel yourself getting out of the vehicle and getting your gear. Picture the entrance to the game venue. What are you thinking and feeling as you walk toward the doors? Imagine yourself walking through the entrance and feeling cool, confident and ready for the game as you look around.

With practice, imagery can be one of the best tools in your mental toughness toolbox. It can be done anywhere, has powerful effects and its applicability is endless! You can learn more about using imagery in Chapter 9.

"Once I got 27/5 I wanted 30/5 then 31/5 now I want 33/5! I am currently at 32.75/5. Even though ¾ laps don't count as a charter "grade," only 32.5 does, it is still ¼ more than I did previously so that's progress!."

– Loogie Vuitton, age 32, skating 6 years

4

FOCUS ON YOUR FOCUS

"Focus? Is there focus in derby? Is there focus in all that chaos?" — Punching Judy, age 47, skating 10 years

How often have you heard your coach shout, "Focus!"? Does this happen every game? Every practice? It's a word that is used frequently in sports when an athlete appears to be having an off moment or an off day. A coach may say this when their skater seems to be spacing out, paying attention to the wrong thing or talking during practice. In post-game interviews on TV, an athlete may explain his or her team's loss by saying, "We just lost our focus out there." Focus is obviously very important for sports. It may even be the most important mental toughness skill. So what exactly is focus?

There are three elements of focus. Selective attention, concentration and attentional control. *Selective attention* is the ability to choose the most appropriate thing to focus on. In a game there is a LOT going on. There are announcers, music, the crowd, the opposing skaters, your own skaters, the opposing jammer, your jammer, your coach, your pivot, what strategies or plays you should be using, the refs…phew! In order to play your best derby you need to figure out which things you should be focusing on and which things are distractions.

Concentration is the ability to sustain attention over time. It isn't very effective to your game if you are focusing on the right elements of the game but aren't holding it in your head long enough for it to be helpful. For example, say you are the jammer and your coach sends you out with instructions to pass the star. You, being the enthusiastic jammer that you are, head out on the track fully planning to do what your coach asked. However, as soon as you hear the jam start whistle, your coach's words are forgotten. You get caught up in the moment and start playing your own game, not what your coach felt was best for the team. You head back to the bench ready for your high five and feel bewildered when your coach asks what happened to the plan. Initially, you were focused on the right thing, your coach's instructions, but you weren't able to sustain your attention to the instructions long enough for them to be put into action.

Attention can be thought of like a flashlight beam. When you hold a flashlight you can aim it here or there. That is selective attention. What you are aiming at is what you are focusing on. You can aim the beam for a long time in one particular direction or shift it back and forth rapidly. That is concentration. You can also move your flashlight closer or farther away from an object, lighting up a larger area or smaller area. Our focus does this as well. Sometimes we have a broad focus, paying attention to many things at once. Sometimes our focus is very narrow and we are totally dialed into one detail. So far your flashlight beam has only been shining on external things but we can also focus on or pay attention to internal elements. These are our thoughts, feelings, beliefs, attitudes, and fears. Focusing on internal things means paying attention to what's going on in your head and body.

Having *attentional control* means being able to mentally shift from external to internal, broad to narrow, and back as appropriate. Choose what is important and stay focused on it as long as necessary. Then shift your focus as needed. Figure 4.1 shows the different dimensions of attention. A pivot needs to be able to develop a broad-external focus of attention because she needs to be aware of the entire playing field. A skater playing the enforcer position, on the other hand requires a much narrower type of concentration to be able to block a particular skater on the other team.

The changing demands of a game necessitate shifting between different dimensions of attention. When a jammer steps up to the jammer line at the beginning of the jam she needs to have a fairly broad-external type of attention. She needs to be able to take in lots of different kinds of information including the position of the opposing blockers, the position of her blockers and the positioning of the opposing jammer. Once the jammer has gathered all of this external information she shifts her attention to a broad-internal focus to plan her attack. She may be thinking of what worked for her previously in the game or in a similar situation or what strategy to employ given what is happening at that point in the game. Once she has her plan, the jammer would shift to a narrow-internal type of concentration to monitor her body to make sure she is set in the best way possible for her attack. She may mentally rehearse her initial explosion into the pack. The jammer might picture in her mind what she wants to feel and see as she bursts forward at the start of the jam. Finally, her attention would shift to a narrow-external focus as the jam whistle blows and she starts doing her thing. All of her concentration at this time would be on the immediate job. Any attention given at this time to other external or internal cues would only interfere with her being her badass self.

- We use a broad-external focus when we are assessing the situation.

- We use a broad-internal focus when we are analyzing our plan of attack.

- We use a narrow-internal focus when we are mentally rehearsing our next move.

- We use a narrow-external focus when we perform our move.

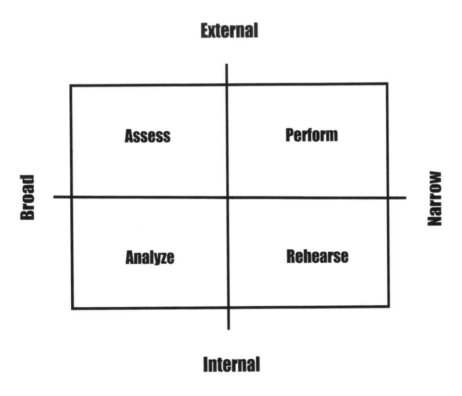

Figure 4.1 Dimensions of Attention

Ways To Improve Attentional Control

Recite key phrases to yourself. Determine what element of the game you want to focus on and remind yourself over and over. All self-talk should be positive, instructional and motivational. So if you have had problems getting back on defense fast enough because you are getting in a hitting war with an opposing blocker you could tell yourself, *Hit, hit, hit, look.* This will remind you to check on how close the opposing jammer is every couple of seconds. You will have time to drop what you're doing and get ready for defense. It doesn't take the jammers long to come around the track again!

Ideas for focusing reminders:	
Defense	Fast Feet
Kill	Ready
Steady	Decide
Now	Power

Remain centered in the present. Our ability to focus effectively suffers dramatically when we aren't in the present. When our minds are time traveling to the future or the past our head is not where it should be — in the game. This can happen for lots of reasons but commonly can be caused by a game not going our way. We can get stuck in the past on mistakes or bad calls that happened earlier in the game and this can prevent us from putting the right amount of focus on what we need to be doing right now. A bad game can also cause us to be focused on the future. Even though it hasn't happened or may not happen we may have already decided we have lost. We may be playing out the results of our loss in our heads —time traveling to the future— which will cause us to play in a way that ensures that we do lose.

"Out or down, out or down."

— Wombpunch, age 26, skating 4 years

Try this: Narrow-To-Broad-External Exercise

This exercise will help you to be able to shift your attention from a narrow-external focus to a broad-external focus. Extend both arms in front of you with your thumbs and forefingers in 'L' shapes to frame a "central focus" in the distance. See that central focus in as much detail as possible. Now slowly begin to move both extended arms to the side, expanding the visual field in your finger frame. Continue to see the central focus as well as everything in between your fingers. This exercise will help you to be able to see your main focus on the track while also being able to pick up the broader field.

> *"My focus changes throughout the game. First few jams it is on the opponents, who is our threats, jammers and blockers. This way I can decide with my team what strategy we need to execute to shut them down and come out victorious. Mid – game, depending on the score, my focus can be on strategy, getting lead, or receiving a star pass if needed. Second half, if we have a good vibe and it is in our favor, my focus is to have continuity each jam, that continuity would be awesomeness.*
>
> *If we are not so victorious, I try and focus on how I can eliminate their biggest threat by way of drawing penalties or playing strong defense against them, one on one. Above all, my focus is communicating with my team because poor communication makes for sloppy play and grumpus mumpus skaters!"* – LoogieVuitton, age 32, skating 6 years

Three Focusing Errors

We all make errors when focusing. One error is having our flashlight beam too broad. This is when we are focusing on way too many things at once. Our performance suffers when we weaken the intensity of our focus and spread it too thin by focusing on irrelevant things. Narrow your focus to the essential elements of the game and your performance will improve. If you are paying attention to the announcers and the crowd your focus is too wide. Essential elements of the game include the jammers, blockers, refs calling your number, game situations and coach's instructions. Non-essential elements include the crowd, the announcer, your opponent's tats

and so on. We only have a limited amount of mental energy so keep your focus concentrated where it's needed and don't let it get diluted!

Another focusing error is to have your flashlight pointing in the wrong direction. This happens when we are totally focused on the wrong thing and are missing crucial elements of the game. Say an opposing skater is talking shit to you on the track and you decide to make it your mission to bring her pain and make her sorry. While this can help motivate your aggression and help your game it can also give you harmful tunnel vision. You may be so involved with tracking that skater that you miss an opportunity to block for your jammer or aren't in position in time to play defense.

Failure Focus

Coaches, friends, family, teammates and fans can cause a *failure focus* in skaters by repeatedly asking questions such as "Why did you do that?" or "What happened out there?" when a skater makes a mistake or fails to live up to their expectations. This type of questioning can cause the skater to become overly focused on what they did wrong instead of what they need to do to perform correctly.

A last focusing error is having your flashlight beam too narrow, or being unable to shift it rapidly enough from one spot to another. An example of not being able to shift focus fast enough is when you are so overly focused on the opposing jammer in the pack that you get taken out by her blockers. A skater needs to be able to divide her attention among all the relevant cues that need to be processed at the same time. A defensive blocker needs to be aware of the positions of both the opposing jammer and her blockers, or be able to rapidly shift attention between them. That way she can adjust her position to be able to continue to attack the jammer instead of being on the floor.

"If the crowd is booing me, like if it's somebody else's crowd, I focus more on the boos than yays, because it means you're doing something right. It encourages me to do it more."

— Punching Judy, age 47, skating 10 years.

Stress Narrows Our Focus

When we are stressed it narrows our field of awareness. This is due to the flight or fight response. The body and mind eliminate unnecessary functioning in order to channel resources to where they are needed most. Our field of vision narrows. Our hearing becomes more sensitive. Our thought processes become simplified. A certain amount of stress is good for our performance. However, if we become too stressed our focus becomes so narrow that we can't function optimally. We want to be aware of our energy levels and be able to adjust accordingly to maintain an optimal level of focus. This graphic demonstrates that without enough stress our focus is too broad, but with too much stress our focus becomes too narrow. We want to be in the middle area which is just right.

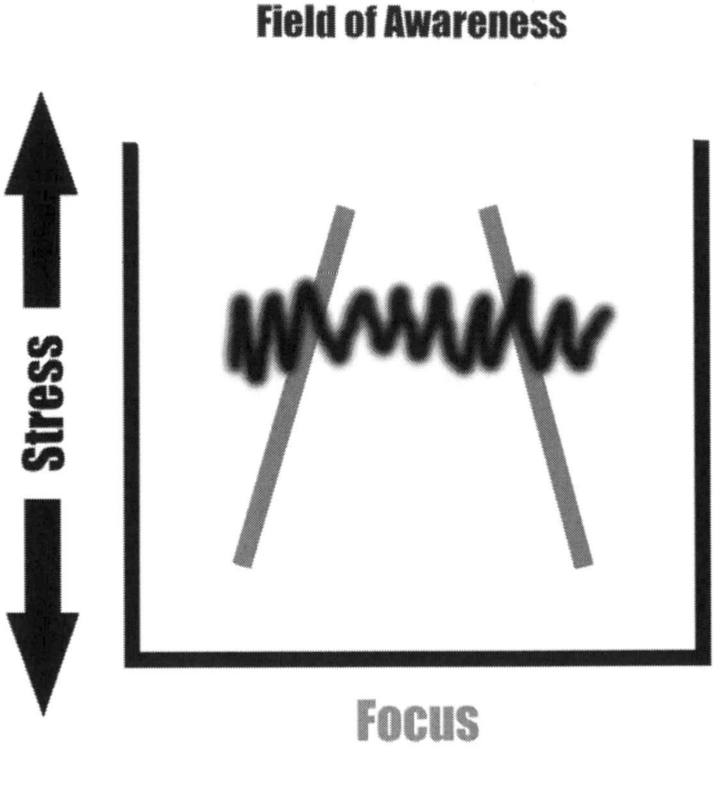

Field of Awareness

Figure 4.2 Effects of Stress on Your Focus

Focus In Sports Is Multisensory

We use many of our different senses when focusing. We use our vision to see what is happening around us. We use our hearing to listen to what refs, coaches and our teammates are saying to us. We use our sense of touch to feel things like non-verbal signals from our teammates, illegal hits from opponents, whether our muscles are tensed correctly or whether our skates are adjusted right. We may even involve our sense of smell and taste. With all of that different sensory input happening it is important to be able to train our brains to be able to put our focus on the right things and eliminate unnecessary distractions. We only have a limited amount of mental energy and we want to put all of it into those elements that are going to allow us to play at our very best.

Try this: Improve Auditory Focus

During a game there are a lot of competing sounds. There may be music, an announcer, refs, coaches, your pivot, opposing skaters, fans and teammates all vying for your auditory attention. Practice training your auditory attention to be able to focus it where you need it.

Sit quietly at home and close your eyes. Try to pick out individual sounds from in and around your house and try to figure out where they are coming from. You might hear people's voices, the sound of the refrigerator or cars passing by outside. Now bring your auditory attention only to those sounds that are inside the room you are in. Tune out anything else. Next bring your auditory attention only to those sounds outside of the room. Then try to hear all of the sounds simultaneously, letting them blend together without trying to differentiate them. Finally, pick out just one sound and bring it to the forefront of your awareness, tuning out all of the other sounds.

"I focus on trying not to die!"

— Pinktastic, age 31, fresh meat

Try this: Improve Mental Focus

1. Focus on the star in Figure 4.3 until everything else disappears.

2. Think only about the star, noticing all of its details.

3. If distractions appear, gently bring your focus back to the star.

4. Don't actively try to shut out disruptive thoughts or feelings, just notice them and then bring your attention back to the star. You can also visualize pinning your distractions to a light fluffy cloud that you can watch float away.

   This skill of being able to "lock in" your concentration can help with the pre-jam nerves that lead to choking. Skaters can transfer that narrow, external focus to the next move they need to be making. This is why tennis players will focus in on the strings of their racket just prior to a serve.

Figure 4.3 Jammer Star Focusing Target

Try this: Scanning And Recognition To Improve Visual Focus

   Take 100 small squares of paper and write the numbers 1 to 100 on them. Next take the pieces of paper and stick them to the wall, randomly in rows of 10. Have someone time you trying to touch a consecutive set of 10 numbers as fast as possible. You could do 20 to 29, 70 to 79, etc. Alternately, you can see how many consecutive numbers you can touch in one minute. This exercise helps your eyes and mind scan and recognize information, therefore strengthening the ability to quickly pick out essential and non-essential pieces of information.

Once you get pretty fast at this activity you can step up the difficulty level by adding distractions such as loud music or somebody trying to get your attention by talking to you. You can also simulate game nerves by doing 10 burpies before you try the activity. The physical activity will increase your heart rate which is one of the physical manifestations of anxiety.

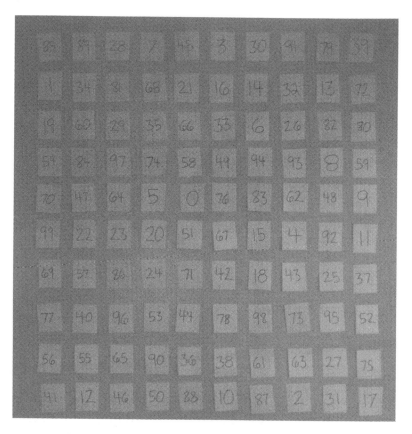

Scanning and Recognition Activity

Try this: Determine Eye Dominance

Finding out which of your eyes is dominant can help you to be extra alert when you are set up with the jammer on your non-dominant side. Make a small triangle, about an inch wide, with both hands. Hold your triangle out in front of you and focus on a small object across the room, placing the object in the center of your triangle. Close your left eye and see if the object remains in view. If so, your left eye is dominant. Close your right eye. If the object remains in view then your right eye is dominant. This is called the Miles Test.

The Miles Test

"I've gotten knocked over because I was daydreaming or being distracted by watching the different techniques people were using."

— Pinktastic, age 31, fresh meat

Understanding Your Best Focus

To improve your performance you need to understand how your focus affects your performance. Sports psychologist, Terry Orlick (2008), suggests that when you understand what works well and what interferes, you can work on improving the consistency and quality of your focus.

- Think of your best performance.

- What were you focused on before the game?

- What did you focus on seconds before you started to play?

- How would you describe your focused feeling during the game?

- What were you focused on during that game?

- Did you ever lose your focus?

- If so, what did you do to get it back on track?

- If not, what kept you focused?

Now think of a disappointing game. If you did feel focused, even for a little while, what did you do to feel that way? If you never felt focused, what kept you from feeling it? Once you find out what works for you and what doesn't you can make a plan to keep your focus as unwavering as possible by influencing those factors that are within your control.

5

DEFEAT DISTRACTIONS

*"If there's a negative vibe happening, I get frustrated and I
don't play as well." — Wombpunch, age 26, skating 4 years*

The mental toughness skill that separates great athletes from the rest is the ability to adapt, refocus and stay positive in the face of distractions. There are so many sources of distractions during a game that becoming sidetracked at some point is inevitable. Distractions can be both internal and external. Winning can be a distraction. Losing can also be a distraction. Teammates, coaches and officials can be distractions. Our thoughts and feelings can be a distraction. Unexpected events can be a distraction. Even changes in your performance level during a game can mess with your head.

What has distracted you from skating at your best? In this chapter you will learn what distracts you, how you can minimize distractions and how to get back on track when you get distracted.

A wide focus of attention is necessary most of the time in a sport like roller derby. But a skater must adjust her focus as needed. As a jammer approaches the pack, her focus needs to narrow. She need to focus on finding holes, anticipating what the blockers are going to

Inattentional Blindness

Coaches can cause skaters to have something called inattentional blindness. This happens when the coach gives the skater specific directions such as, "Watch out for that number 72, she keeps opening up the inside for their jammer." While the instructions are certainly pertinent, this type of exact instruction can narrow a skater's focus too much and they can miss important cues. The coach's instructions can restrict the skater and be distracting.

do and be aware of her own position and technique to avoid penalties and injuries. Even in the pack, the jammer will widen, narrow and shift her focus continually. Sometimes she will be in an intense battle with a single blocker; sometimes she will be approaching a wall of several blockers. She may shift from a narrow focus, concentrating on executing a juke, to a wider awareness of where the opposing jammer is so she can call the jam off at the appropriate time. As the jammer exits the pack her focus will become more broad. This is an opportune time to do things like check the jam ref to see if they have your score correct, remind yourself if you have lead or not, check the time on the clock for those final game changing jams, check the bench for instructions and make strategic decisions.

> *Don't think. Hit.*

As a skater of any position, have you ever been so focused on your own piece of the game that you missed important things going on? Have you ever been so internally focused that you weren't aware of the bigger picture around you? Say a blocker is getting bumped out of bounds repeatedly by a skater on the opposing team and becomes too internally focused. She may start thinking things like *This sucks so much!* or *I wish this jam would end!* She may also start focusing on how tired her muscles are. The blocker may become so distressed that she makes a careless error like accidentally cutting in front of a skater on her re-entry. She may also miss the fact that the opposing jammer just skated by her. She missed an opportunity to make a hit! The blocker's focus was too narrow-internal and should have been more broad-external. She wasn't aware enough of other skaters' positions or the best strategy to be using at the time. She needed to shift her attention out of her own head and onto the track. Her own thoughts and feelings became a distraction.

> *They say the jammer has the glamour but the jammer also has the added pressures of having all eyes on them.*

We usually think of focusing only on external things like the opposing jammer or game strategy. But focusing on internal elements plays a big part as well. Things we focus on internally include our attitudes, our body awareness, our self-talk and our emotions. A successful skater will be able to adjust the amount of focus that is internal vs. external when appropriate. Practice is a time to be more internally focused. When learning new skills we break things down and have a list of mental instructions we tell ourselves as we execute the skill such as, *bend the knees, shift your weight,* and *outside edge.* In a game we don't want to skate the same way we do at practice. Practice is for learning. Games are for performing. Games are for showing what you know. It is not the time to think, but to do. It's the time to trust in your training and in yourself and go for it.

> *"I don't remember a solid distraction when first skating.*
> *Once the whistle blows all I hear is the refs and my*
> *teammates. I don't get distracted by fans or announcers. I*
> *used to get distracted if we were losing when the strength*
> *score is in our favor. Bottom line, I want to win."*

> — *Loogie Vuitton, age 32, skating 6 years*

Choking Under Pressure

Choking is when an athlete plays worse than they are capable of in high pressure moments. Why does choking happen? Skilled athletes do their thing using a streamlined system of brain circuitry that bypasses the prefrontal cortex — the part of the brain that is in charge of things like decision making. This means that what they do is largely outside of their consciousness. They are able to do amazing things without thinking about them because they have overlearned their skills to the point where performing them is second nature. They are on autopilot. In high pressure moments athletes may become worried about the "what ifs" or afraid of failure. When they become distracted by this stress their brain system doesn't work the way it should and they start becoming overly aware of themselves. This leads to choking (Tucker, 2012). Another term for this process is overthinking or paralysis by analysis.

An example of a high pressure moment could be the last jam of the game with the two teams tied in score. The jammer in this situation might feel an incredible amount of pressure because the game is on the line and one wrong move will allow the other team to take the win. She may be feeling afraid she will commit a penalty that will send her to the box. She could also be worried about letting her team down. In an attempt to pull off an amazing jam she tries to analyze and control every aspect of what she is doing. This attempt at increased control ends up backfiring because it disrupts what would normally be a fluid, automatic performance.

The cure for choking under pressure lies in being able to distract yourself from thinking about what you are doing. You need to get out of your head by intently focusing on a mundane detail in your immediate environment like the seam on the shirt of the blocker in front of you. Even the simple trick of singing a verse from a song can help because it prevents the parts of the brain that might interfere with your performance from taking over.

Refocus After Someone Gets Hurt

After witnessing a serious injury it may be difficult for a skater to get their head back into the game. They may be worried about getting hurt themselves or hurting someone else. They may be replaying what they saw happen in their head. If you're going to be on the track, it is important for you to be able to put those thoughts out of your mind and focus on playing the game. It is dangerous to play while distracted because it can be almost guaranteed that at least one of the skaters on the other team will be focused on their game. You need to be ready for them!

Don't Put Energy Into Things That Are Outside Your Control

As has been mentioned, there is a LOT going on in a game. Trying to focus on all of it decreases your performance. What if you're not sure what you should be focusing on? One way to decide what you should put your energy into is to determine what is under your control, what is under your influence and what is outside of your control.

In general, what is under your control are your own thoughts, attitudes and actions. Many people believe that their actions and reactions are not under their control. People sometimes say things like, "It's just how I am," or "I can't help it." However, with mental toughness training you can learn to be the master of your own self. Everything we say, do or think can be controlled. If our patterns aren't working for us we can change them. If your pattern is to walk into a game venue, spot a zebra you've had problems with in the past and instantly feel disgruntled, then you have put yourself and your focus off of playing your best game. Instead of thinking, *I hate that ref! She always calls me for things I didn't do. This game is going to suck,* you can think, *The refs are gonna to do what they're gonna do. I need to focus on what I need to do.*

What is outside of your control are other people's thoughts, attitudes and actions. This includes how opposing skaters act. They may do or say things you don't like or don't want them to do. You may really want them to quit grabbing you in the pack. But yelling at them or committing your own penalties to make them stop or teach them a lesson is not putting your focus where it should be. Your focus should be on your own game and on what you can control in order to be at your finest.

Things that are under our influence are those things that we can try to plan ahead for and do our best to make go our way, but are not completely controllable. This can include equipment malfunctions. You can do your best to maintain your skates and gear, but sometimes shit happens. Having a skate break during a game can be upsetting and distracting. To deal with things in the realm of influence, plan for the worst but hope for the best. Make a plan for how you would deal with a skate breaking in the middle of a game. How would you want to handle the situation?

Try this: 3 Spheres Of Control

This activity can help you become aware of which factors in roller derby you can control, which you can influence and which are outside of your control. Trying to control the uncontrollable leads to increased stress and frustration, wasted energy and decreased levels of performance. Look at the list of possible factors below and determine which circle in Figure 5.1 they belong in. Try to add more factors to the list!

Possible factors:

- your intensity level during practice

- the actions of fans and teammates

- bad ref calls

- gear malfunction

- who you get to skate with during a jam

- your energy level during a game

- going to the penalty box

- unusual behavior by an opponent

- coach's behavior

- your attitude

Figure 5.1 Three Spheres of Control

"I fixate on one thing I did wrong and it ruins me for the entire practice. It just kind of snowballs. Or I fixate on one good thing and it makes me feel a little overconfident and I screw it up again. I need to work on not fixating so much I guess." — *Paisley, age 21, fresh meat*

Sustain Your Attention During Distractions

Distractions come in all forms during a game. With practice you can learn what tends to distract you and how you can get back on track when it happens. For example, if you know that you get so nervous playing in the first jam of the game you can barely function it would be helpful to make a plan to deal with that. A lot of skaters hate skating in the first jam so much that they will try to avoid it. But acting like this is not helpful to growing as a player, can be frustrating to your coach and is not keeping what is best for your team in mind. So instead of avoidance or temper tantrums, use reframing. In the same way changing the frame around a picture changes the look and feel of the picture, changing the frame we have around a situation can change the way we look at it and how we feel about it. Reframing helps us to look at something in a different, more helpful way.

Instead of thinking of the first jam as a huge, terrible thing that freaks you out, try minimizing its importance. You can tell yourself it's just a "jitter jam," meaning its purpose is to get rid of your pre-game jitters and nothing else. Of course, the first jam of the game is as important as any other jam, but this helps take the pressure off. Another way to reframe the first jam of the game is to think of it less in terms of you and more in terms of the other team. Think of the first jam as your opportunity to feel them out to see what they've got. This will help get you out of your own head and focusing on the opposing skaters. By making the first jam seem less crucial or scary or less about you it will reduce your stress which will free you up to be able to skate an awesome first jam of the game.

Stimulus-Response Theory aka Dress Rehearsal

The idea of using a dress rehearsal comes from the concept that an athlete's great performance is conditioned by external and internal stimuli that exist in the practice environment. The greater the number of different stimuli in an athlete's competition environment compared to her practice environment, the more the quality of her performance will suffer. Stimuli include such things as uniforms, make up, skating surface, track boundaries, lighting, music, announcers, refs and the crowd. According to Stimulus-

Response Theory, an unconscious stimulus such as your practice clothes becomes associated with your great performance at practice. Since this stimulus is not present during a game it can't trigger the excellent performance of your skills. Introducing a new stimulus, such as your game uniform, may even inhibit your performance.

If you tend to perform better at practice than during games, take a look at introducing as much game stimuli as possible into the practice environment during the week leading up to a game. It would be impractical to have every practice exactly replicate a game experience, but some of the elements can be brought in. Don't save that boutfit for game day!

Unconscious Stimulus $\longrightarrow$ Response

Try this: TIC-TOC Strategy

Beating yourself up when you become distracted with unproductive thoughts, feelings or actions only adds to your being off your best focus. Instead, accept that it is going to happen and come up with a strategy to quickly get back on track.

The TIC-TOC strategy uses the words TIC and TOC to trigger you to notice when you are having any self-talk, thoughts, or ideas that are irrelevant or off target and then quickly make changes. Anything negative, unhelpful or not on target for attaining your goals would be a TIC. Using this strategy, you would then immediately change your focus to a positive outcome or actions needed to move towards that outcome. The words TIC-TOC cue you to be able to swiftly switch to a relevant, helpful focus.

TIC-TOC.

Try this: Reset With A Centering Ritual

When distracted, take the time to get back on track. You might think, *When on earth would I have time to do this?* With practice you will only need a couple of seconds to get re-centered and get your head back in the game. Take the moments before a jam starts, while you are on the bench waiting to go out on the track, during official reviews or during timeouts to reset. To do this take a deep breath in and out. When breathing in make sure you are filling the diaphragm. If you put your thumb in your belly button and rest your hand on your belly this is the place you want to fill with air. Breathe in, and when you breathe out say a word or phrase to yourself to refocus.

When you breathe out, be sure to completely empty your diaphragm. As with all self-talk, keep it positive, instructional and motivational.

Ideas for refocusing words or phrases

- Let it go

- What's next?

- This moment

- Attack

- Reset

- Go get 'em

Make It OK To Make Mistakes

The Liberty Mutual Responsible Sports program has a motto, "Mistakes are OK." Even though their program is targeted to children, adults also struggle with issues of perfectionism, competitive pressures and being able to deal with making mistakes. Many athletes report that they lose concentration after making a mistake. Some skaters can't forget about what just happened or can't stop stressing about what they think will happen. Dwelling on past mistakes keeps you from focusing on what you need to be doing right now. Worrying about making mistakes in the future keeps you from performing your best at this moment. Thinking about mistakes can be a huge distraction.

Park it. One method for quickly refocusing after a mistake is to *Park It*. If you are dwelling on a mistake, eliminate the thoughts by "parking" them until after the game or practice is over. Tell yourself, *Park It!* Later you can go back and deal with the issue by "unparking" it.

Accept that mistakes will happen. Mistakes are part of playing at 100%. If you are trying too hard not to screw up, your focus is on what you *don't* want to do instead of on what you *do* want to do. Give

yourself permission to mess up and you will free yourself to play at your full potential.

Immediately turn failure into success. As soon as possible after making an error you should mentally rehearse executing the same skills perfectly. Avoid self-judgment or blaming others which disrupts your concentration. Learning is only possible when you make mistakes.

Make sure you have a supportive practice environment. Practice should be the space for learning and that means making mistakes. Being screamed at or put down by teammates or coaches is never acceptable. Part of the improvement process means taking risks and pushing yourself out of your comfort zone. This is not going to be a perfect process and mistakes will be made along the way. If your practice environment is negative, hostile or non-supportive of your learning in any way take the appropriate steps to fix this. It is your league too and you have a right to feel safe to grow there.

There's No Sorry in Derby

Some skaters, especially when first starting out, tend to constantly apologize. We are all learning in derby and the little mistakes that get made during the learning process are no reason to say you're sorry. *Sorry* is one of those golden words that shouldn't be overused. Save the apologies for things you actually should feel sorry for like if you accidentally break your teammate's nose.

"To get back on track I narrow my focus on one thing with higher intensity, usually the jammer."

— Wombpunch, age 26, skating 4 years

Try this: Create A Refocusing Plan

Make a list of all of the things that typically distract you during a game. Next to each one write down what your usual reaction is and why you don't want to continue that pattern. Finally, write down what your new response is going to be and how that will help your game. Figure 5.2 shows an example of a Refocusing Plan.

Make a refocusing plan to deal with potential distractions such as:

- Worries about competitors

- Pre-game hassles

- Stressful game scenarios

- Worries about getting injured

- Disagreement with the coach

- Being close to fouling out

- Crabby teammate

- Not feeling well

> "You have your coach screaming at you from the sidelines and screaming at you and screaming at you. It kind of distracts you from what you need to be focusing on — the game, getting that jammer and hitting her and holding walls and playing offense when I need to and not making holes for people to go through." — EMTease, age 33, skating 5 years

Distraction:	Past response:	How this hurt my game:	New response:	How this will help my game:
Playing against people I have a personal grudge with.	Felt tense, became overly concerned with winning, felt overly critical of my own performance, as if my opponent was judging me.	Did not have focus where it should have been which is on teamwork.	Treat all opponents as if they are the same, tell myself I am a worthy person whether or not my team wins or loses.	I will have more fun, will not be self-conscious, will be more in tune with my teammates.
Seeing that we are down in points towards the end of the game.	I lost my motivation.	I had a hard time giving it my all.	I will get energized to battle back from behind by screaming with a teammate. I will stop looking at the scoreboard and focus on the next move.	I will be able to give 100% effort and will be proud of myself.

Figure 5.2 Refocusing Plan Example

Distraction:	Past response:	How this hurt my game:	New response:	How this will help my game:

Figure 5.3 Refocusing Plan Worksheet

Try this: Breath Counting

Breath counting is a Zen practice that allows you to clear your mind of distractions. It is a deceptively simple technique that requires complete focus.

Gently close your eyes and take a few deep breaths. Then let the breath come naturally without trying to influence it. Ideally it will be quiet and slow, but depth and rhythm may vary.

1. To begin the exercise, count *one* to yourself as you exhale.

2. The next time you exhale, count *two*, and so on up to *five*.

3. Then begin a new cycle, counting *one* on the next exhalation.

Never count higher than *five*, and count only when you exhale. You will know your attention has wandered when you find yourself up to *eight*, *12*, or even *19*.

Perfection is a myth!

6

MANAGE YOUR ENERGY

*"I need to have mental energy more than physical energy. I
trust my skates and trust my skill. I need to have the mental
energy to outsmart and be two strides ahead of my opponent
but still have mental control enough to be one with my
teammates on the track. If I am angry I skate awful, if I am
too happy I get silly and distracted. I have resting bitch face
on bout day. I have never been asked, "What's wrong?" so
often on a single day in my life. I call it resting focus face!"*

— Loogie Vuitton, age 32, skating 6 years

The mental toughness skill of energy management has to do with
raising or lowering our arousal levels as needed in order to play at our best.
Arousal, also referred to as pressure or stress, often gets a reputation as
being something bad that we need to eliminate from our lives. However,
some level of stress is absolutely necessary in order for us to get anything
done.

The Inverted-U Graph (Figure 6.1) shows the relationship between our
performance and the amount of pressure we feel. If we have low pressure
we aren't going to have a good performance. If you come into a game
clearly knowing you are going to dominate the other team it is extremely
difficult to garner enough energy to play your very best. You are most
likely going to be playing at some percentage of your full potential,
matching what you are giving to what you are getting. The opposite is also
true. If you are too stressed or overwhelmed you are also not going to be
able to skate a great game.

As pressures rise so does your performance. But only to a certain
point. After that, adding any more pressure causes your game to fall off.
The amount of stress a skater needs to perform at her best is different for
each person. If a skater is high strung and intolerant of stressful situations

even a small amount of pressure is going to put her over the top of the inverted-U curve. If a skater has a very calm, cool and collected personality she will be able to tolerate a lot more stress before it negatively impacts her performance. This skater may need to use psych-up techniques to get energized enough to perform optimally. Mastering the mental toughness skill of energy management means finding out what works for you and then trying to make it happen as often as possible.

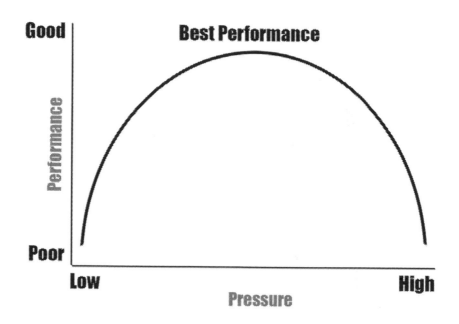

Figure 6.1 Inverted U Graph

Harnessing The Pre-Game Butterflies

Most of us get butterflies in our stomachs or feel our hearts racing before a game. The way we interpret these physical feelings is crucial to how we are going to perform. We can either interpret the feelings as fear that we aren't going to skate well or as a sign that we're ready to go. How we think we are going to play is directly related to how we actually play.

These physical feelings come from the *flight or fight response*. Our mind perceives danger and is preparing us for battle! Our minds can't distinguish between real and imaginary danger or emotional and physical danger, and we will have the same physiological reactions. The hypothalamus sends a message to our adrenal glands and suddenly we can hear better, see better, jump higher, think faster and hear more acutely. Some of the danger we will meet on the track is very real so our minds aren't totally incorrect.

Having to pee or poop is part of the same flight or fight response that is triggering the increased heart rate and butterflies. We get rid of excess weight to make us leaner and meaner. Once we go to "fight" mode all non-essential functions, including digestion, stop so resources can be directed to muscles and other essential areas. Have you noticed that once you start playing that need-to-pee-every second feeling disappears?

We usually interpret these physical stress responses as a negative thing, saying to ourselves, *I'm so nervous about the game!* or *I'm not ready for this* or *I'm freaking out!* We relate the physical feelings to all sorts of negative thoughts such as fear of failure, not being able to manage our emotions, fear of messing up or fear that we will let our family or teammates down.

> *When you feel those pre-game jitters think to yourself, "Good! I'm ready."*

We can learn to think of these physical feelings as helpful and necessary rather than harmful. If you aren't at all concerned about the game you probably aren't going to perform well. You can come to realize that you want to feel this way. The nerves bring out the best in you.

Other physiological responses to stress that you might feel before a game are tension in the neck and shoulders, queasiness, shaky legs, sweaty palms, loss of focus, hot flashes or a feeling of being out of control. These responses are not helpful and will take away from your performance. As an exercise to see how excessive muscle tension can affect speed and coordination try the following:

Place your hand on the table with the palm down and the fingertips touching the surface (like Thing in the Addams Family). Tense all of the muscles in the hand and fingers and try to alternately tap each fingertip on the table as fast as possible. Now relax all of the muscles in the hand and fingers and try it again. You will notice a

> *Strap some skates on those butterflies and kick some ass!*

huge difference in the speed and agility of your movements when your muscles are relaxed as opposed to tense.

"When I get to practice I think 'oh it's gonna be so hard and I'm going to have to work out. And when I get done it's like, 'oh that was awesome.' I need to think about how I'll feel after the practice, like how much I've learned and how good I feel. That's actually what gets me to go. I need to focus on how good I'm going to feel after and how much closer I'm going to be to getting to play." –Paisley, age 21, fresh meat

Try this: 4-7-8 Relaxation Breathing

When you are stressed your breathing will be short, shallow, and irregular. Smooth, deep, rhythmic breathing indicates confidence, calm and control. One method of breath control is to inhale for a count of 4, hold it for a count of 7 and exhale for a count of 8. Be sure to breathe deeply, filling and emptying the diaphragm completely. If you put your hand on your belly you should feel your hand moving in and out as your diaphragm fills and empties.

- Close your mouth and inhale quietly through your nose to a mental count of **four.**

- Hold your breath for a count of **seven.**

- Exhale completely through your mouth, making a whoosh sound to a count of **eight.**

- This is one breath. Now inhale again and repeat the cycle three more times for a total of four breaths.

"If I talk to a teammate that helps ground me a little bit."

– Wombpunch, age 26, skating 4 years

Effects Of The Flight Or Fight Response On The Body

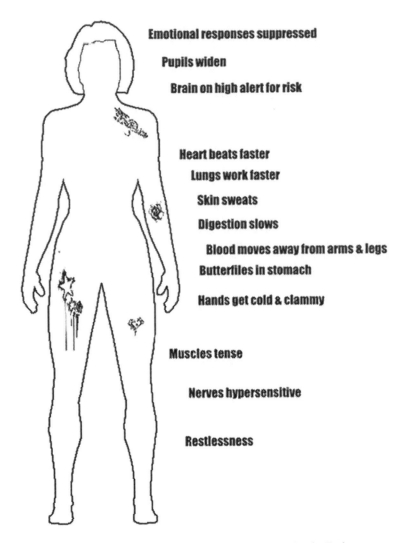

Emotional responses suppressed

Pupils widen

Brain on high alert for risk

Heart beats faster

Lungs work faster

Skin sweats

Digestion slows

Blood moves away from arms & legs

Butterflies in stomach

Hands get cold & clammy

Muscles tense

Nerves hypersensitive

Restlessness

Figure 6.2 Effects of the Flight or Fight Response On the Body

Here are some ways to tame that pre-game anxiety if it's getting out of control:

Smile. It's hard to be upset when you are smiling. Smiling takes the edge off the pressure. It helps keeps things in perspective. Roller derby is supposed to be fun. Enjoy yourself!

Listen to music. Bring some music and listen to it before the game. Make sure to put on tunes that make you feel calm.

Stay focused on the present. Become totally immersed in your pre-game routine. Check your gear, eat your pre-game snack, do your warm up and so on. with complete focus and concentration. Pay attention only to the immediate work in front of you. Thinking about what can happen later in the game will increase anxiety.

Use social supports. Surround yourself with positive, relaxed people before the game. These can be friends, family, teammates or coaches. If you see them handling the situation with cool confidence it will help you to react the same way.

Use self-talk. Telling yourself things like *Be here, Calm,* or *Breathe* can help to get you grounded when your anxiety is spinning you out of control.

Get a massage. Stress tends to give us muscle tension in the neck and shoulders. Get one of your derby sisters to give you a quick massage to help you loosen up.

Find a quiet place. Take a walk by yourself around the outside of the venue or find a quiet corner to spend some time alone. Even sitting on the can will get you a few moments to yourself.

> *"I am really comfortable at saying 'hey, my head's not in this game' and letting someone else go in. I've been able to learn someone might be on and I might be off and I'm one of the first people to recognize it and I might just pull myself out of a couple jams and reassess where I'm at."*
>
> *— Punching Judy, age 47, skating 10 years*

Pacing

An important aspect of energy management is pacing. When a skater knows how to pace themselves they can play at a steadily high level of energy for the entire game. Pacing involves knowing how much energy is required of you for a game, self-awareness about how much stored energy you have and being able to dole out your energy in appropriate amounts throughout the game so you don't run out before it ends. Effective pacing also means not wasting energy on unnecessary things and being able to create more energy if you need it.

Using self-awareness and experience, a skater can learn their own signs of feeling sapped or having a ton of energy left. The skater can then adjust the way they are playing the game in order to be the best they can possibly be for the entire game. Skaters can also learn how to store away the excess energy they have before a game for use later on. This is an excellent way to make use of the pre-game jitters. To do this, create a mental picture of the energy you have. Now visualize yourself taking that energy and placing it somewhere inside of you where you will be able to draw on it later. During the game when you need more energy, tap that source!

One source of energy drain is muscle use. A skater may be using too much muscle tension for a particular situation. For example, a newer skater may not yet have the strength to be able to skate a long, physical warm up and then be strong for an entire game. This skater should conserve her energy for when it is needed. Or a jammer may go so balls out on her first few jams that she doesn't have anything left to be able to jam the rest of the half. Another source of energy drain is overreacting to an official's call, anger, frustration or worrying about the performance of yourself or your teammates. Anger, frustration and worry are emotions that tend to interfere with skating your best. Skaters can learn how to transfer the energy that comes from anger and frustration into useful energy that can help them to accomplish their performance goals. One way to do this is through self-talk. A skater who feels super pissed off can tell themselves they are going to transform their *Anger into strength, Anger into speed,* or *Anger into agility.* Repeating phrases like these will manifest your desires into reality.

Another way to gain energy is to take it from your environment and put it to your own use. Here are some potential places you can find energy:

- The opposing team

- The crowd

- Your teammate

- Your coach

Try this: Create A Relaxing Mantra

Come up with a phrase that you can say to yourself when your nerves have got the best of you. Take a deep breath in, filling your lungs. Then slowly empty your lungs while you say your mantra to yourself. Repeat as necessary.

Here are some ideas:

This is what you've trained for.

You've got this.

It's not about me, it's a team effort.

Cool and calm.

Try this: Progressive Muscle Relaxation

This is Edmund Jacobson's progressive relaxation technique. Progressive relaxation is based on three assumptions:

- It is possible to learn the difference between feeling tense and relaxed.

- You can't be tense and relaxed at the same time.

- Relaxation of the body will lead to relaxation of the mind.

In each step you'll tense a muscle group and then relax it. Pay close attention to how it feels to be relaxed as opposed to tense. For each muscle group, perform each exercise twice before progressing to the next group. As you gain skill, you can omit the tension phase and focus just on relaxation. Listen to a recording of yourself reading the instructions or have someone read them to you for maximum benefits.

1. Find a quiet place, dim the lights, and get in a comfortable position with your legs uncrossed. Take a deep breath, let it out slowly, and relax.

2. Raise your arms, extend them in front of you, and make a tight fist with each hand. Notice the uncomfortable tension in your hands and fingers. Hold that tension for 5 seconds; then let go half way and hold for an additional five seconds. Let your hands relax completely. Notice how the tension and discomfort drain from your hands, replaced by comfort and relaxation. Focus on the contrast between the tension you felt and the relaxation you now feel. Concentrate on relaxing your hands completely for 10 to 15 seconds.

3. Tense your upper arms for 5 seconds and focus on the tension. Let the tension out halfway and hold for an additional 5 seconds, again focusing on the tension. Now relax your upper arms completely for 10 to 15 seconds and focus on the developing relaxation. Let your arms rest limply at your sides.

4. Curl your toes as tightly as you can. After 5 seconds, relax the toes halfway and hold for an additional 5 seconds. Now relax your toes completely and focus on the spreading relaxation. Continue relaxing your toes for an additional 10 to 15 seconds.

5. Point your toes away from you and tense your feet and calves. Hold the tension hard for 5 seconds; let it out halfway for another 5 seconds. Relax your feet and calves completely for 10 to 15 seconds.

6. Extend your legs, raising them about 6 inches off the floor, and tense your thigh muscles. Hold the tension for 5 seconds, let it out halfway, and hold for another 5 seconds before relaxing your thighs completely. Concentrate on relaxing your feet, calves, and thighs for 30 seconds.

7. Tense your stomach muscles as tight as you can for 5 seconds, concentrating on the tension. Let the tension out halfway and hold for an additional 5 seconds before relaxing your stomach muscles completely. Focus on the spreading relaxation until your stomach muscles are completely relaxed.

8. To tighten your chest and shoulder muscles, press the palms of your hands together and push. Hold for 5 seconds; then let go halfway and hold for another 5 seconds. Now relax the muscles and concentrate on the

relaxation until your muscles are completely loose and relaxed. Concentrate also on the muscle groups that have been previously relaxed.

9. Push your back into the chair or floor as hard as you can and tense your back muscles. Let the tension out halfway after 5 seconds, hold the reduced tension, and focus on it for another 5 seconds. Relax your back and shoulder muscles completely, focusing on the relaxation spreading over the area.

10. Keeping your torso, arms, and legs relaxed, tense your neck muscles by bringing your head forward until your chin digs into your chest. Hold for 5 seconds, release the tension halfway and hold for another 5 seconds, and then relax your neck completely. Allow your head to hang comfortably while you focus on the relaxation developing in your neck muscles.

11. Clench your teeth and feel the tension in the muscles of your jaw. After 5 seconds, let the tension out halfway and hold for 5 seconds before relaxing. Let your mouth and facial muscles relax completely. Concentrate on totally relaxing these muscles for 10 to 15 seconds.

12. Wrinkle your forehead and scalp as tightly as you can, hold for 5 seconds, and then release halfway and hold for another 5 seconds. Relax your scalp and forehead completely, focusing on the feeling of relaxation and contrasting it with the earlier tension. Concentrate for about a minute on relaxing all of the muscles of your body.

Cue-controlled relaxation is the final goal of progressive relaxation. This means once you become skilled at relaxing your muscles you will be able to quickly achieve this state using a cue word. Breathing can serve as the impetus for making this happen. Take a series of short inhalations, about one per second, until your chest is filled. Hold for 5 seconds; then exhale slowly for 10 seconds while thinking to yourself the cue word, *relax*. Repeat the process at least five times, each time striving to deepen the state of relaxation you are experiencing.

> *"It's a matter of learning how to control the adrenaline. Oh my god learning how to control the adrenaline is huge because if you're not used to sports you're not used to that."*
>
> *— Punching Judy, age 47, skating 10 years*

Try this: Rainbow Body Scan

The Rainbow Body Scan is a quick way to use imagery to assess and rid the body of any excess tension. You can do this quick technique once you've become adept at recognizing muscle tension through the progressive muscle relaxation exercise above:

While you are standing, imagine a wide beam made up of every color of the rainbow is moving over your body, starting at the top of your head and moving all the way down to the bottoms of your feet. Imagine the rainbow traveling over and through your body, having the ability to see inside of you. As the rainbow moves across each area, notice if there is any tension there. If so, take a deep breath in and as you breathe out, release the tension.

Try this: Five Finger Relaxation Technique

The five finger relaxation technique (University of Chicago, 2014) only takes a few minutes and can help you with pre-game anxiety. By reducing the mental effects of anxiety, you will reduce the physical effects of anxiety.

a. Touch your thumb to your index finger. Think about a time when you felt healthy fatigue, like after an exhilarating scrimmage. Imagine how good it felt to have used everything you had physically without overdoing it. Your body felt good, your muscles strong.

b. Touch your thumb to your middle finger. Recall a time you felt loved. You may have experienced a hug or an intimate conversation. Remember how nice and warm it felt to have the support of someone who was important to you.

c. Touch your thumb to your ring finger. Think about a time you exerted special effort. Someone noticed and gave you a sincere compliment. Hear the words and feel gratitude that someone acknowledged your contribution.

d. Touch your thumb to your pinky. Imagine the most beautiful outdoor place you have ever been. You felt satisfied and inspired by the wonders of nature and felt at peace with the universe. Remain there for a while.

Getting Pumped

What if you find yourself without enough energy? You may just not be feeling it that day. But that's just not going to work when you have a game. You will need to have a repertoire of energizing techniques you can use when you need them:

Jump around. Physically moving around will raise your heart rate and your energy level. If it's too early too warm up on the track you can do something off-skates to get your blood flowing.

Listen to music. Queue up a song that puts you in the state of mind you want to be in. Pick a jam that makes you feel happy, hyper, aggressive or whatever it is that you need.

Use your social supports. Surround yourself with people that are in the state of mind you want to be in. If you see a few of your fellow skaters laying around pre-game, skip them and seek out the ones who are hip checking walls or unleashing their inner warrior.

Watch a video. Nothing gets you ready for derby like derby. Put together a playlist of some great video clips showing hard hits and fast action. It doesn't even need to be derby to work. Any inspirational sports video is going to increase your motivation to get out on the track and give it 100%.

"Usually the crowds give me a boost of energy."

— Wombpunch, age 26, skating 4 years

Try this: Create An Energizing Mantra

Muhammad Ali was the king of psyching himself up by talking about himself and his skills. Here are a few of his gems:

"I'm not the greatest, I'm the double greatest."

"I'm so fast that last night I turned on the light switch in my hotel room and was in bed before the room got dark."

"If you even dream of beating me, you'd better wake up and apologize."

Now come up with your own mantra that you can say when you need energizing. Here are a few ideas:

We're going to crush them!　　　　　*We're bringing the pain!*

I'm untouchable!　　　　　　　　　*It's go time!*

Try this: Energy Management Feedback Worksheet

What is your best performance state? Do you need to be pumped up? Do you need to calm down? Completing the Energy Management Feedback Worksheet after games can help you to understand the connection between your energy levels and your performance. Get to know yourself, get to know what works best for you and try to make it a consistent part of your routine.

"I don't like to be extremely intense. I kind of like to be in the middle somewhere between intensity and kind of calm. I that middle space, that zen space."

–EMTease, age 33, skating 5 years

After playing roller derby, everything else is easy.

Energy Management Feedback Worksheet

What were your stressors for today's game?

How did you experience the stress (thoughts, feelings, actions)?

Rate your performance today:

I played poorly	1	2	3	4	5	I played well
I felt anxious	1	2	3	4	5	I felt relaxed
Muscles were tense	1	2	3	4	5	Muscles were loose
I felt tired	1	2	3	4	5	I felt energized
I was distracted	1	2	3	4	5	I was focused

My energy level was (circle one):

    too low   just right   too high

I used this technique to energize:

I used this technique to relax:

Energy Management Feedback Worksheet

7

THINK POSITIVELY

"When I first started it was, 'what am I not doing well' and now it's, 'what can I be doing better?'"

— Wombpunch, age 26, skating 4 years

The ability to make the power of your thoughts work for you is a mental toughness skill that you will be able to utilize both on and off the track. In this chapter you will learn how to recognize, challenge and modify unhelpful, faulty or negative thinking that is holding you back from meeting your full potential in both derby and in life.

It is necessary to first have a good understanding of the differences between thoughts, feelings and actions. *Thoughts* are the beliefs, attitudes, perceptions and ideas we have in our heads. *Feelings* are the emotions and sensations we have in our bodies and hearts. *Actions* are the things we do or say. Here are some examples of some thoughts, feelings and actions:

Thoughts: *I can't do anything right, I'm going to get hurt, Things are going my way, I hate her, I can handle this.*

Feelings: Happy, confident, sad, worried, excited, disappointed.

Actions: Punch someone, avoid people, stop trying, smile, walk away.

Our thoughts lead to feelings which then lead to actions. For every situation we encounter we immediately have a thought about it. This thought then leads us to have an emotional reaction. We may feel

> *If your friend talked to you the way you talk to yourself, how long would you remain friends?*

happy, angry, fearful or sad. This feeling will then influence our actions. You may think, *I don't trust people.* This will make you feel anxious which will cause you to avoid others. The interplay between these three elements is happening continuously as each moment we are encountering a new situation. Situations can be either internal or external. An emotion can be a situation that you react to.

Body responses

Along with thoughts, we have physiological responses to situations. Our hearts may pound or we may feel dizzy when we perceive something amazing is happening. We may feel heavy or our chest may ache when something sad is happening. We may feel headaches or stomach aches when we interpret our situation as stressful.

In Figure 7.1 you will see that the situation the skater is thinking about is having to skate on a concrete floor. Her initial thought is *I never play well on concrete.* This thought leads her to feel nervous prior to the game. Feeling nervous then causes the skater to play with hesitation and hold back. By changing that thought to a more helpful one she is able to get to her goal of playing to the best of her ability. When encountering the concrete floor she instead thinks, *The best teams in the world compete on concrete.* This leads her to feeling the courage she needs to be able to play aggressively.

> "When I first started it was 'Breathe, breathe, breathe, move your feet, breathe, breathe, breathe', and now it's, 'Hey what do I need to do in this next jam to help out my team' or 'Oh she's going back out and I need to remember to do this or that.' Its changed from a very 'Do this, do this, do this, breathe, breathe, breathe' to 'Oh hey you need to go out and take care of her." — Punching Judy, age 47, skating 10 years

Think Confidently

Some sports psychologists believe that confidence is a result of how we think more than our physical talents, opportunities or past success. *Self-talk* is a word used to describe some of the things that we think. Self-talk is the stuff we tell ourselves. It acts as a mediator between an event and our response to the event. Self-talk has a huge impact on how we react to situations. Negative self-talk will disrupt your concentration, destroy your confidence and be detrimental to your performance. Self-talk can even affect your body by causing your muscles to tense when you think stressful thoughts or relax when you think calming thoughts.

An injured skater who has experienced a setback in her recovery may think, *I'll never get back on the allstar team.* This thought will make her feel hopeless, angry, tense and frustrated. The skater can notice she is thinking negatively and use negative thought-stopping to halt this thought and change it to a positive one like, *This type of injury takes time to heal, I need to work hard at it.* This thought will lead her to feel optimistic, calm, motivated and have increased effort.

Negative self-talk can take the form of mean words or pessimistic predictions. Skaters may tell themselves some pretty horrible things — things they wouldn't even say to their worst enemy! Or they may tell themselves things they wouldn't put up with hearing from others. Think about the words, *I suck!* Would you tell someone on your team that they sucked? Would you put up with someone on your team telling you that? The messages we repeatedly hear become the fabric that makes up who we believe we are. We don't always have control over what others say to us but we can control what we tell ourselves. Be your own best supporter!

Skaters may also tell themselves negative things in the form of predictions about what is going to happen. If a jammer tells themselves, *I'm never going to get through* or *She's going to kill me!* then that is what is likely to

---

Emotional Honesty

There are four core emotional wounding experiences that humans endure: loss, rejection, betrayal, and humiliation (Brain Works Project, 2014). We can learn to cope with crappy feelings by using emotional honesty to figure out what is really important to us. When we feel a *loss* it can help us learn how much we really love or need what has been lost. When we feel *rejection* we can understand how much we want to be accepted. When we feel *betrayal* we know how much people we trusted or respected hurt us. When we feel *humiliation*, our sense of self is devastated because we want to belong.

happen. Our thoughts can create a powerful self-fulfilling prophecy. When you think it, it is more likely to occur so why not bank your money on how you really want the future to be.

The other danger in making negative predictions is that they can create a vicious cycle of reinforcement. Imagine you are a blocker and a super squirrely jammer is coming at you. Say you make a negative prediction such as, *She's going to skate right past me.* If the jammer does skate around you as if you were standing still, your negative prediction will be reinforced. *See, I knew she was going to skate right past me.* When you find yourself in a similar situation you will be more likely to make a negative prediction. This pattern can drag you further and further away from your derby goals. Why not create an upward spiral instead of a downward spiral? Same scenario, same squirrely jammer approaching, instead think, *I can stop her.* If you stop her then you have just reinforced the habit of making optimistic predictions. If you don't stop her don't go back to negative patterns, continue to think positively and eventually your thoughts will become reality.

Balancing acceptance and change

Sometimes our negative self-talk comes from the idea that we aren't "enough." We may believe we aren't fast enough, skinny enough, big enough, strong enough, cute enough, smart enough... good enough.

Accept yourself as you are right now. You are exactly as you should be at this moment in time. As you accept that you are "enough" right now, simultaneously work on areas you want to improve.

Have the serenity to accept the things I cannot change,

The courage to change the things I can,

And the wisdom to know the difference

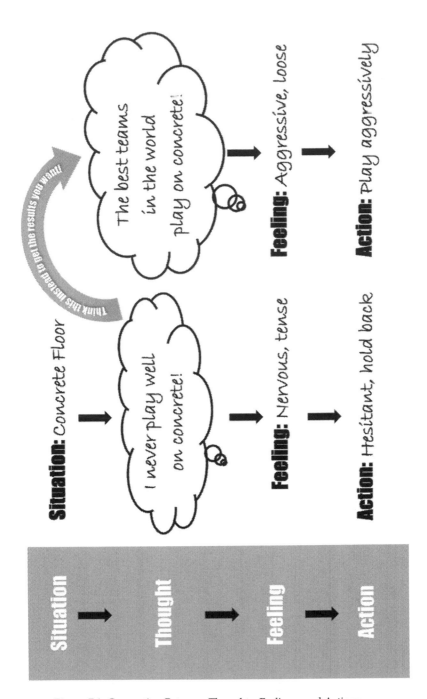

Figure 7.1 Connection Between Thoughts, Feelings, and Actions.

Skaters need to throw away their mean, negative self-talk such as:

I'm so stupid.

I'll never make it.

I don't deserve to be on this team

And replace it with supportive, positive self-talk like:

I'll keep getting better if I just work at it.

I can beat her.

Just keep calm and focused.

Negative self-talk is anxiety producing, causes self-doubts, and gets in the way of making your derby dreams a reality. Once you start to monitor your thinking you can begin to transform your self-talk so that it is working for you and not against you. One technique to stop negative thinking is to simply tell yourself, *Stop,* and then immediately replace the negative thought with a positive one.

Speak kindly to yourself! Positive self-talk should provide encouragement and motivation and should not be judgmental. You may think self-talk such as, *You call that a hit!* is pushing you in the right direction, but this type of self-talk has a critical tone that can be hurtful. Replace it with something like *Hit through her, do it now!* Be sure to state things as what you want to do, instead of what you don't want to do. If you tell yourself *Don't blow it!* You're brain and body are going to remember *Blow it!*

Having confidence is not a you-either-have-it-or-you-don't situation. Start working at noticing, stopping and changing negative self-talk to positive self-talk while you are at practice. Then you will be more likely to be able to do it in a high pressure game situation. You will begin to learn which situations produce negative thoughts and why that might be. In time, by managing the way you think, your self-confidence will grow.

Whose voice is it that you hear in your head?

"I've gotten to the point where I can reset between jams. You say, 'Ok that didn't go so well you need to try something else." And it might take two jams to get there. Or three. But I've gotten to the point where I can reset."

– Punching Judy, age 47, skating 10 years

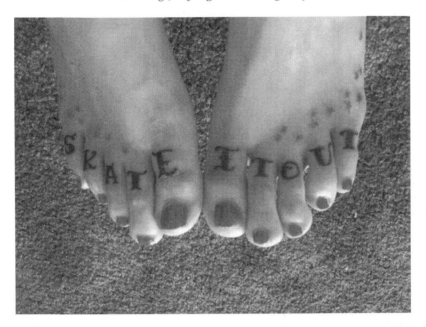

"Skate it out!" – Loogie Vuitton, age 32, skating 6 years

Red Flag Words

Red flag words such as *never, must, hate, should, have to,* and *always* can create a black and white thinking pattern that can increase a skater's anxiety or anger. We create our own reality with our thoughts. Red flag words are limiting and give us a very narrow way of thinking. If we think skaters on the other team *shouldn't* ever block us illegally then we are going to get upset when it happens. This anger and frustration is going to distract us from playing our best game. If we instead accept that illegal hits are a part of derby then we have eliminated a trigger. There's a reason we get multiple trips to the penalty box!

Here are some examples of ways red flag words can be changed to open up possibilities rather than shutting them down. Say the sentences out loud and notice how simply changing a word or two can evoke different feelings. The red flag words and the words they are transformed into are in bold:

1. *I **hate** it when I get called for something I know I didn't do!*

Transform this into: *I **don't like** it when I get called for something I didn't do, but it's going to happen sometimes.*

2. *I **never** get through when I jam.*

Transform this into: ***Sometimes** I get through when I jam.*

3. *The coach **should** play me more.*

Transform this into: ***It would be great** if the coach played me more.*

4. *I **have to** make the allstar team.*

Transform this into: *I really **want to** make the allstar team, but I will live if I don't.*

> *"I show disappointment in myself because I know I can do better so when I don't hit hard or I miss the jammer and they go by me I tell myself 'you should have caught them, you should have been paying attention' or 'you need to be more watchful or you need to get where you need to be and get in that wall and hold that wall.' So I kind of discipline myself. It makes me realize where my weaknesses are."*
>
> *— EMTease, age 33, skating 5 years*

Try this: Changing Negative Self-Talk To Positive Self-Talk

Use the worksheet (Figure 7.2) to practice changing negative self-talk to positive self-talk. Make a list of all the negative self-talk that hurt your performance or made you act in an undesirable way. Now create a corresponding positive self-talk next to each negative one. Make sure these are realistic and things you would actually tell yourself. You have to believe these things!

For example:

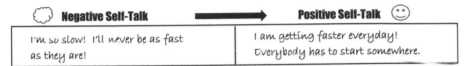

Negative Self-Talk	Positive Self-Talk
I'm so slow! I'll never be as fast as they are!	I am getting faster everyday! Everybody has to start somewhere.

Faulty Thinking Styles

Faulty thinking styles can be broken down into categories. Most of us use some faulty thinking at some point. It is usually an automatic response outside of our awareness. When it becomes problematic is when we constantly use these styles of thinking. It can lead to emotional distress, interpersonal problems and get in the way of achieving what you want to in derby. Here are a few of the most common faulty thinking styles (adapted from Kliethermes, 2009):

"Drama Queen Jean" (Catastrophizing). Jean blows everything out of proportion. Even if it is a really small problem she acts like it's the biggest deal in the world. She may end friendships over things others think are not a very big deal. She is quick to get angry and slow to forgive.

"Emo Emily" (Emotional Reasoning). Emily makes decisions based on her emotions. She thinks, *If I feel it, it must be real.* Emily was feeling irritable at practice one day and decided one of her teammates was super annoying.

"All of Nothing Nancy" (All-or-Nothing). Nancy only sees the world in terms of black and white, or good and bad. Nancy doesn't see shades of grey. She came in third place during a skating race at practice and thought, *I suck!*

"Over and Over Olive" (Overgeneralization). When something bad happens to Olive, she thinks it will happen again and again. Because one of the skaters on the opposing team cussed at her, she is sure they are all bitches.

"Psychic Sue" (Mind Reading and Fortune Telling). Sue makes assumptions about what others are thinking without really knowing. Sue will then make decisions based on those assumptions. She saw a photo of some of her teammates hanging out without her on social media and thought, *They didn't invite me, they don't like me.* Sue then purposefully did not invite those same teammates to drinks the next week. Sue will also predict the future, like when she knew she was going to hate practice because her teammate was leading even though her teammate had never coached before.

"Not a Big Deal Danielle" (Magnification and Minimization). Danielle magnifies the positive achievements or attributes of other people while minimizing her own positive achievements and attributes. At the same time, she sees her mistakes or faults as huge and those of others are seen as insignificant. She hardly notices when a teammate misses a block but when she does it she feels like she blew the whole game.

To begin to change these faulty thinking patterns we need to first recognize that we are thinking in an unhelpful or negative way. This means increasing our self-awareness. Think of a situation where you used one of the faulty thinking styles above. What were the thoughts that went through your mind? What feelings did you experience as a consequence of your thinking? What actions did those feelings lead to? Did those actions lead you closer or farther away from your derby goals?

"Balance, focus, calm."

— Wombpunch, age 26, skating 4 years

"'I'm getting a lot stronger and will be faster.' I can see the differences in my body and my shape and stuff, how much more fit I am now than when I started. It puts me in the positive mind set I need rather than if I break myself down which I have a problem doing."

–Paisley, age 21, fresh meat

> *Never let negative possibilities enter your mind. Only think about how amazing it's going to be when you pull it off.*

89

Try this: Write Your Own Horoscope

Horoscopes tell people what will happen in their future and guide an individual's behavior so they can make the best of it. Don't leave it up to the stars! Write your own horoscope for what you want to happen in your future and create your own destiny. Expecting something will happen makes it more likely that it will actually happen so keep it optimistic!

Example of a horoscope for practice:

You will enjoy dynamic cooperation from your teammates tonight. Things that seemed impossible in the past will suddenly appear effortless. Be on the lookout for positive changes in others. There's an unmistakable passion in the air that will grant you more zest for life!

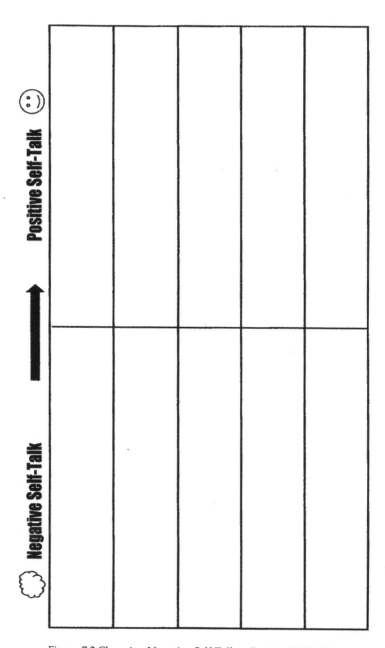

Figure 7.2 Changing Negative Self-Talk to Positive Self Talk.

Challenging Self-Doubts

Sometimes it may be difficult to battle self-doubts because we really believe they are accurate. This is especially true when our attitudes and beliefs have been with us since childhood. In order to begin to restructure our thinking patterns we need to be as objective as possible. Self-doubts are often about worries, fears or insecurities. *I'll never get it, I'm the worst one on the team, I'm going to get hurt, I can't do it,* or *I'm stupid* are all examples of self-doubts. The following exercise will help you to challenge and reframe self-doubts.

1. First, uncover any self-doubts you might have about yourself:

"_____."

2. Second, challenge your belief by asking yourself questions such as:

What's the worst thing that could happen?

What is the evidence?

Is there another way of looking at things?

3. Finally, replace your faulty belief with a new belief. One way of coming up with a new belief is by asking yourself:

What would I tell my best friend if she said the same thing?

Another way of coming up with a new belief is to ask yourself what belief is going to get you where you want to be.

New belief: "_____."

8

CREATE CONFIDENCE

What is confidence? Confidence is the belief that you can get the job done, whatever it may be. Confidence is probably the mental toughness skill that skaters crave the most, and with good reason. An important factor that distinguishes highly successful athletes from less successful athletes is confidence. Top athletes have a strong belief in themselves and their abilities. So how does confidence make you a better skater?

Confidence affects game strategies. The less confident you are feeling, the more reserved your game strategies are going to be. When you are feeling confident you are more willing to implement bold strategies because you will believe you can pull them off.

Confidence increases effort. The more confident you feel the more motivation you are going to have. You will believe your efforts are going to pay off.

Confidence affects psychological momentum. Confidence can create an upward spiral of momentum that can carry you to great heights. When you are feeling confident you will be able to play better and this, in turn, will give you more confidence.

Confidence affects performance. Without confidence you will hold back, hesitate and paralyze yourself with overthinking. With confidence you will perform with fluidity and freedom.

Confidence helps you focus. When you are feeling confident you are not going to be distracted by self-doubts, worries, frustration or other things that negatively affect your game. The task at hand will receive your full attention.

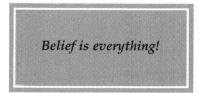

Belief is everything!

Confidence gives you positive emotions. Lack of confidence gives you negative emotions such as disappointment, fear, jealousy, distrust and anger. Confidence makes you feel joyful, proud, fulfilled and optimistic.

> *"Confidence is the key to playing derby because it's a contact sport. But at the same time derby has helped me build my confidence." — Punching Judy, age 47, skating 10 years*

Where Does Confidence Come From?

Confidence comes from several sources, both internal and external:

- Feeling comfortable in the environment

- Seeing things going your way

- Demonstrating your ability

- Seeing other skaters performing a skill

- Trusting in the abilities and decisions of your coaches and teammates

- Getting support from teammates, coaches, family and friends

- Feeling good about one's body

- Physical and mental preparation

- Feeling healthy

- Developing and improving skills

Lack of confidence can come from many places as well:

- Fear of what people think of you

- Fear of failure

- Fear of success

- Fear of injury

The biggest source of self-confidence is past accomplishments. If you succeeded at something in the past you will think you can do it again. Conversely, if you failed at something in the past, you won't believe you can do it in the future.

Coaches can set up practices so that skaters can experience the success that leads to confidence. Coaches can run drills for a variety of skill levels during practices. Also, skaters can set small goals for themselves that they are able to accomplish. For example, *I can skate 11 laps in two minutes. Next time I'm going to go for 11 and ¼ laps in two minutes.*

> *"Being that fit has given me confidence because I know I look better. I know I'm fit so even like walking down the street it's like, 'You want to mess with me? No you don't.' I don't cross the street to avoid people. It's definitely given me confidence in that way."* — Punching Judy, age 47, skating 10 years

Types Of Confidence

Overconfidence. Overconfidence is when one's confidence is greater than their abilities. This is being falsely confident. It is not overconfidence if your confidence is based on actual skills and ability.

Lack of confidence. You have lack of confidence if you have the physical skills to be successful but are not able to perform these skills under pressure. Self-doubts undermine your performance by creating anxiety, breaking concentration and causing indecisiveness.

Optimal Self-confidence. Your confidence is at an optimal level when you are so convinced you can achieve your goals that you will strive hard to do so. Optimal self-confidence is essential to reaching your potential. Figure 8.1 shows the relationship between performance and confidence. As your confidence goes up, so does your performance. However, if you become overconfident your performance does not keep pace. You will perform the best under optimal self-confidence conditions.

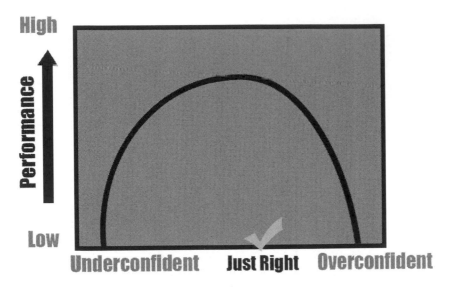

Figure 8.1 Performance-Confidence Graph

The Self-Fulfilling Prophecy

The Self-Fulfilling Prophecy is a scientifically proven phenomenon whereby expecting something to happen actually causes it to happen. As the figure of the vicious cycle of the negative self-fulfilling prophecy shows, when we expect failure and then fail, our self-image is lowered and this then increases our expectation of future failure. Since this is a cycle, one can enter it through any of the pathways. For example, having a low self-image can lead to increased expectations of failure. Or experiencing failure can lower our self-image.

> *Some self-doubt is good because it helps maintain motivation and prevents contentment and overconfidence.*

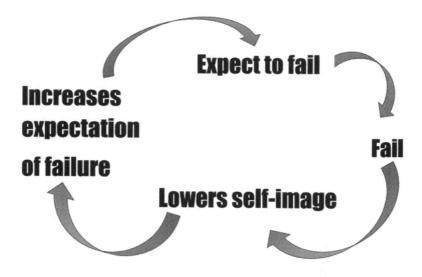

Figure 8.2 Vicious Cycle of the Negative Self-Fulfilling Prophecy

 A great example of overcoming a negative self-fulfilling prophecy is the story of Roger Bannister. In 1954 Bannister broke the four-minute mile barrier. Before this time, runners agreed that it was impossible to run a mile in less than four minutes. Bannister believed he could do it...and he did. An even more incredible part of this story is that the next year more than a dozen runners broke the four-minute mile. What happened? Did runners suddenly become faster? Nope. What happened was that the runners finally believed that it could be done.

Try this: Battling Confidence Killers

Think of some things that have wrecked your confidence during a game or practice. This could be something a coach or teammate said or a situation that occurred. Why did it negatively affect you? Our thoughts about a situation lead to us having feelings which then cause us to act in certain ways. An example of confidence killing thoughts leading us away from our goals follows. The connection between thoughts, feelings and actions is covered in more detail in Chapter 7.

Situation: My coach looked unhappy with me when I came off of the track.

Unhelpful Thought: *I did terrible! I hope I don't have to jam anymore this game.*

Negative Feeling: Disappointed in myself.

Unwanted Action: Avoid jamming if possible.

One way to address these confidence killing situations is to start with what you want to be able to do and go backwards. What is the action you want to have? If you want to be able to jam then what is the feeling you would want to have in order to be the most successful? You would want to feel confident. What thoughts would make you feel confident? Next we have the same situation but we have changed our thought to a more helpful one that gets us where we want to go.

Situation: My coach looked unhappy with me when I came off of the track.

Helpful Thought: *That jam didn't go as well as I wanted it to but I can do better next time.*

Positive Feeling: Confident that I can do well on my next opportunity.

Desired Action: Get out there and jam!

It is essential to point out that the skater's perceptions of the coach's thoughts and feelings might not even be accurate. Sometimes we tend to play the role of mind reader and put our own ideas about what people are thinking and feeling into their heads.

It is also important to note that we are focusing here on changing the elements of this situation that we have the most control over. Instead of putting our energy into making our coach change his or her behavior, we are focusing on changing our own thoughts, feelings and actions to be in line with our goal of being the best skater we can be.

Now you can try it. Think of a confidence killing situation and fill in the worksheet according to how you reacted in thoughts, feelings and actions. Then take the same situation and replace the thought with a more helpful one. You will know if you did it right when all three elements (thoughts, feelings and actions) are aligned and lead you to where you want to be.

Situation: _____.

Unhelpful thought: _____.

Negative feeling: _____.

Unwanted action: _____.

Situation: _____.

Helpful thought: _____.

Positive feeling: _____.

Desired action: _____.

*"My confidence has soared tremendously. When I first went
to open recruitment, I walked in after puking, with my head
down and very scared. I was afraid to do anything by myself.
I didn't want to be looked at or judged or made fun of. I've
always came off as this super cool, confident, and loud person
but secretly I was shy and afraid. Defense mechanism I guess!
Derby has taught me that you should never be ashamed of who
you are. It has built me up physically (derby ass and thighs),
mentally, and intellectually. I owe my cool factor to derby!"*

— Loogie Vuitton, age 32, skating 6 years

Try this: Self-Confidence Test

For each of the items decide if you feel underconfident, confident, or overconfident. After you have completed the test look over your answers to see which areas need focus.

1. Your derby skills.

2. Your ability to make critical decisions during a game.

3. Your ability to perform under pressure.

4. Your teammates.

5. Your ability to let go of distractions.

6. Your ability to find energy when you need it.

7. Your ability to control your emotions during a game.

8. Your coaches.

9. Your ability to stay focused.

10. Your team's ability to come back when behind.

*"We were skating and I jumped the cones with both of my feet
for the first time. Then the entire practice was just awesome
cuz I was like 'oh can't break me down now'."*

— Paisley, age 21, fresh meat

Acting Confident

Acting confident has to do with our body language and facial expressions. The more confident a skater acts, the more likely she is going to feel confident because of the interplay between our thoughts, feelings and actions. You can influence your thoughts and feelings by changing your actions. Our actions are what we say and do. So by acting confident, we actually become more confident. This is also important because when a skater appears to lose confidence their opponent will see this and gain confidence.

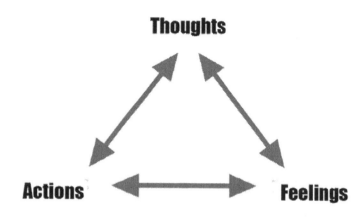

Figure 8.3 Interplay of Thoughts, Feelings, and Actions

We have all seen a demoralized jammer. This is a jammer who looks physically and emotionally cooked. Everything about them looks defeated —from their posture to their facial expression. They may stop before entering the back of the pack, not wanting to go forward. They may appear limp when skating. Their speed slows. They take too long to get up off of the floor. They just look like they've given up. Even if you are feeling this way, don't show it on the outside. Instead, act confident. Keep your opponents guessing by keeping your game face on and your posture strong. BOUNCE off of that floor and keep coming at them!

Have you ever seen one of your teammates giving everything they've got to get the jammer? How does that affect your game? For most skaters it will make them want to keep trying as well. The opposite is also true. If you see your teammate letting the jammer go while still in the engagement zone then you may give up too. Much of this is communicated by body language. So think about the influence you want to have on your teammates. Do you want them to give it everything they've got? If so, then that starts with you. Other opportunities to make a show of confidence are walking into the game venue as the visiting team or skating off the floor at halftime when your team is down in score.

Acting confident can actually lead to true confidence. Fake it until you make it. The confidence to keep fighting, to give it 100% can be communicated to your teammates and to yourself through your body language.

> *"When I'm on the line and I look back at the jammer and you usually get a brief moment of eye contact and that's my 'game on' moment. I get to show them that I'm not scared and I know what I'm doing."*
>
> *— Wombpunch, age 26, skating 4 years*

Try this: a S.W.O.T. Analysis

A S.W.O.T Analysis (Figure 8.4) can help you increase your confidence by assisting you to identify your Strengths, Weaknesses, Opportunities and Threats.

In the strengths box list all of your strengths. In the weaknesses box list your weaknesses. The top row is all about internal elements, so the strengths and weaknesses you list should be ones that are inside of you. List your opportunities and threats in the corresponding boxes. The bottom row is about external factors, so the opportunities and threats you list are those that are outside yourself. The left column leads to success and the right column contributes to failure. At the end of your analysis you should have both internal and external elements that will lead to your success or failure. By focusing on your strengths, eliminating your weaknesses, overcoming threats and taking advantage of your opportunities your confidence will soar!

Working in a group with others of the same skills level can increase confidence, effort and performance!

"Seeing the morale of others go down, that brings me down."
— *Wombpunch, age 26, skating 4 years*

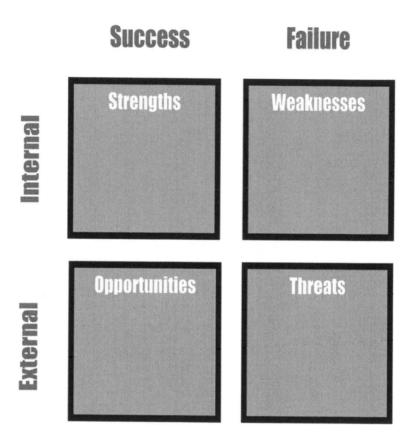

Figure 8.4 S.W.O.T. Analysis

Try this: Locus Of Control Scale

Locus of Control is a theory of personality psychology developed by Julian Rotter in 1954. Locus of control is all about the degree to which individuals believe they can control the events that affect them. Some people feel that events are more controlled by external factors and others think that they have more personal control over events. These different ways of thinking can be seen as occurring on a spectrum. At one end of the spectrum is what is called an *external locus of control* and at the other end of the spectrum is an *internal locus of control*. Most people fall somewhere in between.

Answer the following questions by choosing either (a) or (b) to see where you end up on the Locus of Control Scale:

1. (a) Children get into trouble because their parents punish them too much.

(b) The trouble with most children nowadays is that their parents are too easy with them.

2. a) Many of the unhappy things in people's lives are partly due to bad luck.

(b) People's misfortunes result from the mistakes they make.

3. (a) One of the major reasons why we have wars is because people don't take enough interest in politics.

(b) There will always be wars, no matter how hard people try to prevent them.

4. (a) In the long run people get the respect they deserve in this world.

(b) Unfortunately, an individual's worth often passes unrecognized no matter how hard she tries.

5. (a) The idea that teachers are unfair to students is nonsense.

(b) Most students don't realize the extent to which their grades are influenced by accidental happenings.

6. (a) Without the right breaks one cannot be an effective leader.

(b) Capable people who fail to become leaders have not taken advantage of their opportunities.

7. (a) No matter how hard you try some people just don't like you.

(b) People who can't get others to like them don't understand how to get along with others.

8. (a) Heredity plays the major role in determining one's personality.

(b) It is one's experiences in life which determine what they're like.

9. (a) I have often found that what is going to happen will happen.

(b) Trusting to fate has never turned out as well for me as making a decision to take a definite course of action.

10. (a) In the case of the well prepared student there is rarely if ever such as thing as an unfair test.

(b) Many times exam questions tend to be so unrelated to course work that studying is really useless.

11. (a) Becoming a success is a matter of hard work, luck has little or nothing to do with it.

(b) Getting a good job depends mainly on being in the right place at the right time.

12. (a) The average citizen can have an influence in government decisions.

(b) This world is run by the few people in power, and there is not much the little guy can do about it.

13. (a) When I make plans, I am almost certain I can make them work.

(b) It is not always wise to plan too far ahead because many things turn out to be a matter of good or bad fortune anyhow.

14. (a) There are certain people who are just no good.

(b) There is some good in anybody.

15. (a) In my case getting what I want has little or nothing to do with luck.

(b) Many times we might just as well decide what to do by flipping a coin.

16. (a) Who gets to be the boss often depends on who was lucky enough to be in the right place first.

(b) Getting people to do the right thing depends on ability, luck has little or nothing to do with it.

17. (a) As far as world affairs are concerned, most of us are the victims of forces we can neither understand, nor control.

(b) By taking an active part in political and social affairs the people can control world events

18. (a) Most people don't realize the extent to which their lives are controlled by accidental happenings.

(b) There really is no such thing as "luck."

19. (a) One should always be willing to admit mistakes.

(b) It is usually best to cover up one's mistakes.

20. (a) It is hard to know whether or not a person really likes you.

(b) How many friends you have depends upon how nice a person you are.

21. (a) In the long run the bad things that happen to us are balanced by the good ones.

(b) Most misfortunes are the result of lack of ability, ignorance, laziness, or all three.

22. (a) With enough effort we can wipe out political corruption.

(b) It is difficult for people to have much control over the things politicians do in office.

23. (a) Sometimes I can't understand how teachers arrive at the grades they give.

(b) There is a direct connection between how hard I study and the grades I get.

24. (a) A good leader expects people to decide for themselves what they should do.

(b) A good leader makes it clear to everybody what their jobs are.

25. (a) Many times I feel that I have little influence over the things happen to me.

(b) It is impossible for me to believe that chance or luck plays an important role in my life.

26. (a) People are lonely because they don't try to be friendly.

(b) there's not much use in trying too hard to please people, if they like you, they like you.

27. (a) There is too much emphasis on athletics in high school.

(b) Team sports are an excellent way to build character.

28. (a) What happens to me is my own doing.

(b) Sometimes I feel that I don't have enough control over the direction my life is taking.

29. (a) Most of the time I can't understand why politicians behave the way they do.

(b) In the long run the people are responsible for bad government on a national as well as on a local level.

There are no right or wrong answers to this test and having one locus of control is not necessarily better than the other. However, for achieving your derby best an internal locus of control may serve you better. If you scored higher that means you may believe that your destiny is controlled by external forces including:

Fate   *Luck*   *Powerful Others*

If you scored lower that means you may believe that your destiny is guided by your own efforts and involves such actions as:

Hard Work   *Personal Decisions*

Scoring The Locus Of Control Scale

Do not score items 1, 8, 14, 19, 24, 27

Give yourself one point each for the following (23 points possible):

2b	6b	11a	16b	21b	26a
3a	7b	12a	17b	22a	28a
4a	9b	13a	18b	23b	29b
5a	10a	15a	20b	25b	

Internal ⟵⟶ **External**

There are things you can do to shift to a more internal locus of control. First, recognize that you always have a choice. Making no choice is actually a choice in itself. By making no choice you are allowing other people or events to decide for you. Second, set goals. By working towards your goals you are controlling what happens in your life. Third, develop your decision making and problem solving skills. You will find that with these skills you can get through tough situations. Finally, pay attention to your self-talk. If you catch yourself saying, "I have no choice" or "There's nothing I can do" remind yourself that you do have some control. Feeling like you have control over things gives you confidence!

Interestingly, research has shown that those who have an external locus of control do better in cases of serious illness or injury. It seems that believing the circumstances were not under their control helps people to avoid the self-blame that can hinder recovery.

> *Skaters who say I CAN and act as if this is the case will unfailingly skate at higher levels.*

Try this: Weighing Pros And Cons

Being able to make decisions gives us confidence. One way to make a decision is to weigh the benefits and costs of each possibility. As an example, say you were trying to decide whether or not to travel to an out of town derby training camp. To analyze the pros and cons of this decision you would list the reasons to go in one column and the reasons not to go in another column. Then you would go back and assign a value ranging from 1 to 5 to each of the pros and cons with 1 being the least valuable or important reason and 5 being the most valuable or important reason. Finally, you would add up your totals to see whether you are going to stay home or go to the training camp. The side with the most points wins. It's a lot more helpful than using a Magic 8 Ball!

Here is an example of a pros and cons list:

Question: Should I go to the derby training camp?

PROS	and	CONS
I will meet new derby sisters -3		It is going to cost a lot of money -5
I can bring knowledge back to my team -2		I will need to take a day off work -3
I will learn a LOT! -5		
Total: 10		**Total:** 8

Decision: Looks like I'm going to the camp!

Affirmations

In his book, *Creative Coaching* (2001), sports psychologist Jerry Lynch defines an affirmation as "a strong, positive, concise phrase that states one's goals and directions." The words an athlete uses and hears are often the predictors of future realities. Negative words take away one's confidence by creating anxiety and self-doubt. Watch out for subtle negative affirmations. If you say "I will not cut the track" all your brain will hear is "cut the track, cut the track, cut the track." Instead, say "I will re-enter legally." Your body will do what you tell it to.

"I'm glad my first game is going to be out of town. Not a lot of my family will come to watch. I might look like an idiot because it's my first one." – Pinktastic, age 31, fresh meat

Try this: Power Of Words

To test the power of words Jerry Lynch suggests saying the following phrases out loud:

"I am a strong, vibrant, talented athlete, capable of performing at high levels of excellence."

"I am a weak, worthless, wilted slob who is wasting away in derby."

Notice the difference in how you felt emotionally and physically when saying the two statements. In the first case you should have felt positive emotions such as excitement and motivation. Your posture may have even become straighter. In the second case your body may have drooped down and you may have felt hopeless and defeated.

"I guess I have problems comparing myself to those who are really really good and make it look easy. And it's not. I'm not super confident but I'm getting there."

– Paisley, age 21, fresh meat

Try this: Power Of Words II

Jerry Lynch also suggests doing 10 pushups while repeating "I can do this. This is making me stronger. I love this." out loud over and over. Rest for a couple minutes and then do 10 more pushups while constantly repeating "I hate this. This is so hard. I can't do it." out loud over and over. Did you feel stronger when you were using the positive affirmations?

"Proper hits, holding the walls, teammates saying 'hey good job', constant encouragement, the comfortability of being on my skates. That gives me confidence."

– EMTease, age 33, skating 5 years

Photo by Christopher Chase

Try this: Write Your Own Affirmations.

Affirmations should be short, simple and positive. They should state what you want, not what you don't want. Be sure to use the present tense. This will help you to act as if the future is now. Once you have your affirmation written down, say it out loud every day and act as if it were true.

Here are some examples of affirmations:

I skate 13 laps in 2 minutes.

My ass is my weapon.

I hit harder and harder, every day in every way.

I skate so fast, I'm untouchable.

I am a force to be reckoned with.

Think about having a different affirmation for all of the separate aspects of derby.

Self-image: *I am constantly improving.*

Ability: *I hit like a semi-truck.*

Opponents: *I am in control and ready to roll.*

Confidence: *I'm a rock star.*

Concentration: *I am here, now.*

Injury: *I am healthy, worthwhile and strong.*

Goals: *I achieve success every day.*

3 More Ways To Build Self-Confidence

Physical conditioning. Roller derby takes incredible strength and endurance and knowing you have what it takes will fill you with confidence. Do you have the balance, agility and core strength to take and avoid hits? Do you have the cardio to be able to skate multiple jams in a row if necessary? Do you have the muscle strength to keep your speed and intensity up the whole game? Answering "yes" to these types of questions will ensure that you will go into any game situation with confidence.

Training. Knowing you have a great coach who provides you and your team with the training you need will also build your confidence. Does your coach provide well rounded training that addresses all aspects of derby including rules, teamwork, skating skills and strategy? Do you feel that your coach is providing you with enough attention during practice to be able to help you achieve your personal derby goals? Do you think your coach has the expertise to be coaching? Does your coach seek out new information from coaching resources that are available? Having confidence in your coaching will build your confidence.

No mental toughness training program can take the place of physical skill and conditioning. To achieve your best performance physical training should be integrated with mental toughness training.

Social environment. Your coaches and teammates can have a big impact on your self-confidence. Unfortunately, sometimes that impact can be a negative one. Being yelled at by a teammate, being ignored or put down by a coach or other harmful experiences can be damaging to your self-confidence and make you doubt yourself. Having encouraging, supportive teammates and a coach that can create a positive practice environment can give you the confidence you need to be comfortable enough to take the chances necessary to learn and grow as a skater.

True confidence is based on having control of your perceptions, emotions and behaviors. This type of confidence is very stable and it takes quite a lot to rock it. Confidence that depends solely on coaches, teammates or favorable situations is an inconsistent type of self-confidence. Practicing the mental toughness skills in this book will help you to be able to have true, unwavering confidence. Roller derby requires so much toughness physically and mentally. It is much more extreme than most sports. It can give you inner strength and confidence that lasts for the rest of your life!

9

USE IMAGERY

Imagine you are standing in your kitchen holding a fat lemon in your hand. Feel the bumpy texture. Notice the bright yellow color. Now picture yourself putting the lemon down on a cutting board, picking up a knife and slicing the lemon in half. You can see the lemon's juices rolling off the cutting board. You can smell the strong lemon scent. Now, see yourself cutting off a thick slice of the lemon. Pick up the juicy lemon slice and take a huge bite out of it.

What just happened? If you are like most people, your mouth started watering or puckering as if you had bit into an actual lemon. If so, you just experienced the power of imagery.

Imagery is sometimes called visualization or mental practice. Imagery is probably the mental toughness skill that is the most underutilized or unknown. Imagery can be used for learning and practicing skating skills, correcting mistakes, getting through an injury and more. After reading this chapter you will be able to incorporate this highly valuable tool that can take your performance to the next level.

How Does It Work?

Imagery is a simulated experience that occurs entirely in your mind. It involves vividly imagining yourself performing a skill. When we visualize an image our brain sends impulses to our muscles in the same way actually performing a skill would. Imagined experiences and actual experiences are equally real for the brain. As the experiment with the lemon visualization showed, the body will react the same way to a real and

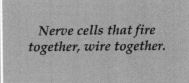

Nerve cells that fire together, wire together.

114

imagined experience! When a skater uses imagery she is using her brain to program her mind and body to do what she wants them to do.

Using Imagery

You can image from two different perspectives. You can see yourself as if you are watching a movie. This external perspective can be changed to view yourself from the front or back, from the top or from the sides, just like a movie camera can move around you. Or you can image from your own perspective, as if you are looking out of your own eyes. Research has shown that internal imagery creates more neuromuscular activity, but both are useful. The best thing to do is practice both perspectives and experiment to find which are most effective for you in specific situations.

In order to make imagery as effective as possible you should make it as realistic as possible. Use as many of your senses as you can. Use your kinesthetic sense to feel the sensation of your body as it moves in different ways. Use your olfactory senses. What do you smell? Do your wrist guards stink? Use your visual senses. What do you see around you? Do you get a glimpse of the jammer's star on her helmet before she ducks into the pack? Use your auditory senses. What sounds do you hear? Is your pivot shouting something at you? Use your tactile senses. What are you feeling? What does your jammer's hand feel like on your arm as you give her a whip?

It is important to involve your thoughts and feelings in your images as well. What are you thinking of when executing the block that knocked the opposing skater to the floor? What emotions do you have when you get past that last line of defense? What thoughts do you have when your team wins a game? What are you feeling when you come off the track after some particularly great teamwork? Increasing your self-awareness will help your images be more accurate and effective.

Always do your imaging in real time. That means if something would take 30 seconds in real life then it should take 30 seconds when you visualize it. The only exception to this would be when you are learning a new skill. It would be okay to imagine yourself doing it in slow motion in order to break down the steps. However, you should work towards speeding the mental practice session up until it matches real time.

The two aspects of effective imagery that a skater needs to master are *vividness* and *controllability*. Vividness refers to how detailed an image is.

One of the features of a vivid image is the inclusion of the emotional experience. It is important that a skater is aware of underlying thoughts and feelings that are influencing her performance. Other aspects of vividness include colors, shapes, involving as many senses as possible and other particulars. Controllability is how well a skater can manipulate her images. Some features of controllability are the ability to correct an error, slow or speed time and adjust the perspective.

You might picture yourself using imagery while lying down with your eyes closed. But this is not necessarily the most effective method for all situations. While learning how to image it may be helpful to minimize distractions and give your full attention to the imaging process. Lying down or sitting in a comfortable position with eyes closed is also appropriate for practicing imagery for purposes such as relaxation. When using imagery for things such as refocusing during a game or mentally correcting an error it can be practiced in a relaxed way at home at first. However, once you get the hang of it, imaging can be done with your eyes open in a chaotic game setting. The best way to utilize imagery to learn new skating and derby skills would be to actually walk through movements off-skates.

Verbal triggers or *symbolic images* can help a skater build a mental picture of their perfect performance. Verbal triggers are words that remind an athlete of certain points they want to focus on or emphasize in order to perform a skill correctly. *Quick feet, Explode up, Soft and hold, Follow through, Turn the shoulders,* and *Weight on the back leg* are some examples of verbal triggers. Notice that they are positive instructions of what you want to do and not what you don't want to do. *Don't skate tall* would not be a good verbal trigger because it puts the focus on incorrect actions.

Symbolic images are mental pictures that a skater can conjure up to give their brains a blueprint of the perfect action they want to perform. A jammer imagining her legs are made of springs, defensive blockers seeing themselves as connected to each other with Velcro, or a blocker imagining she is made of steel are three examples of symbolic images. A skater can make a symbolic image more accessible by actually finding a picture of their image and putting it somewhere they can look at it every day. Coaches should use verbal triggers and symbolic images when teaching you a skill or reminding you of how to perform it correctly. Using these in your mental practice, especially for learning or correcting skating and derby skills, will help make it more effective.

It is vital to visualize yourself doing things correctly and successfully. Often we replay ourselves making mistakes or getting injured. All this does is reinforce those ideas in our brains and bodies. Recall, the brain reacts the same way to real and imaginary situations so make sure you are practicing those skills and circumstances that you want to manifest on the real world track.

"I picture hitting people, hitting them hard. I picture them on the ground and that makes them less scary."

— Wombpunch, age 26, skating 4 years

Try this: Vividness Exercise 1

The following visualization exercises are adapted from those Robin S. Vealey and Christy A. Greenleaf (Williams, 2006) suggest doing to help you develop the vividness and controllability of your images. When practicing

See yourself doing the things you want to be able to do. Mentally practice doing things correctly!

visualization exercises it is helpful to record yourself or someone else reading the "scripts" out loud. That way you can focus on listening to the cues for your imaging rather than trying to read at the same time.

Place yourself in your practice space. It is empty except for you. Stand in the middle of this place and look all around. Notice the quiet emptiness. Pick out as many details as you can. What does it smell like? What are the colors, shapes and forms that you see? Now imagine yourself in the same setting, but this time there are many spectators there. Imagine yourself getting ready to play in a game. Try to experience this image from inside your body. See the spectators, your teammates, your coach and your opponents. Try to hear the sounds of the noisy crowd, your teammates and opponents yelling, your coach shouting instructions and the sound of wheels on the skating surface. Re-create the feelings of nervous anticipation and excitement that you have before competing. How do you feel?

Try this: Vividness Exercise 2

Think about your skates. Try to imagine their fine details. Turn one over in your hands and examine every part of it. Feel it's outline and texture. Feel the laces, the plates, the wheels, the bolts. Now imagine yourself skating around the track. First, focus on seeing yourself very clearly skating. Visualize yourself repeating the strides over and over. See yourself skating from behind your own eyes. Then step outside of your body and see yourself skating as if you were watching yourself on a video. Now step back into your body and continue skating. Next try to listen to the sounds of your skates pushing off the floor. Listen carefully to all of the sounds involved in your skating. Now put the sight and the sound together. Try to get a clear picture of yourself skating and also hearing all of the sounds involved.

Try this: Vividness Exercise 3

Pick a very simple skating skill. Perform this skill over and over in your mind and imagine every feeling and movement in your muscles as you perform that skill. Try to feel this image as if you were inside your own body. Concentrate on how the different parts of your body feel as you stretch and contract the various muscles associated with the skill. Think about building a machine as you perform the skill flawlessly over and over again and concentrate on the feeling of the movement.

Now try to combine all of you senses, but particularly those of feeling, seeing and hearing yourself perform the skill over and over. Do not concentrate too hard on any one sense. Instead, try to imagine the total experience using all of your senses.

Try this: Controllability Exercise 1

Choose a very simple derby skill and begin practicing it in your mind. Now imagine yourself performing this skill either with a teammate or against an opponent. Imagine yourself executing successful strategies in relation to the movements of your teammate or opponent.

Try this: Controllability Exercise 2

Choose a particular skating or derby skill that you have trouble performing. Begin mentally practicing the skill over and over in your mind. See and feel yourself doing this from inside your body. If you make a mistake or perform the skill incorrectly, stop the image and repeat it, attempting to perform perfectly every time. Re-create past experiences in which you have not performed the skill well. Take careful notice of what you are doing wrong. Now imagine yourself performing the skill correctly. Focus on how your body feels as you go through different positions in performing the skill correctly. Build a perfect machine!

Try this: Calibration Exercise

Get your coach or a teammate to help you to calibrate your images. Set up a drill such as jumping the apex. Have your coach or teammate watch you attempt the jump and then immediately describe your jump back to them, mentally recalling your performance. Which foot did you push off of? How did you land? With both feet simultaneously or with a staggered landing? Were you in bounds or out? How many inches were you from the track line? What were your arms doing? Your coach or teammate can then tell you what they saw to make sure your perceptions of what you are doing are accurate.

Using Imagery To Correct Mistakes

As derby skaters we are constantly getting corrections from our coaches. If your coach knows their stuff they will be telling you what *to do* rather than what *not* to do. You should listen to what your coach tells you and then incorporate that feedback into an image that allows you to really see and feel the skill being executed correctly.

Often skaters try to correct mistakes by force and self-badgering. If their coach tells them to keep their elbows in when executing a hit, the skater may mentally yell at themselves something like, *Arrgh, keep your elbows in. I know this! Why do I keep doing this? Quit following with the elbows, stupid!* A more effective way to correct mistakes is through the use of imagery. Use a KISS (Keep It Simple and Systematic) approach. When your coach gives you feedback or when watching yourself make a mistake in game footage, immediately see yourself doing it correctly and feel yourself doing it correctly.

1. Feedback

2. See it

3. Feel it.

Using Imagery To Learn New Skills

Visualization can be used to help you learn any new derby or skating skill you desire. This is an example of how this mental toughness skill can be utilized to help a skater learn how to transition from forwards to backwards while skating.

1. Watch a skilled skater perform a transition. This can be either in person or on a video. Watch them do a transition several times to get an idea of the timing and movements involved. Now close your eyes and imagine the skater performing the transition. Next try to put yourself in the other skater's body and really picture what the timing and movements feel like.

2. Now walk through the transition several times in your sneakers or socks. Pay attention to the timing and the rotation of the feet. Notice how your feet are staggered, one in front of the other. Feel the weight coming off of the heels as you pivot from forwards to backwards on the balls of your feet. Close your eyes and feel yourself performing the transition.

Develop verbal triggers or symbolic images such as these for the various movements involved in the transition:

a. Right foot out.

b. Sit back into skates

c. Tightrope!

d. Light on heels

e. Switch and hold

3. Close your eyes and imagine yourself performing the transition. Concentrate on the thoughts and feelings associated with performing this skill successfully. Imagine yourself transitioning and feeling confident. Use imagery to mentally practice the transition so that it becomes consistent in feeling and timing. Alternate between walking through the transition and imagining yourself performing the transition. Try to feel balanced and in control during both activities. Use your triggers or symbolic images during your mental practice and your walk-through.

4. When you physically perform the transition on skates during your next practice focus on creating the same feelings during the physical performance as the mental practice. Before physically performing the transition imagine yourself successfully doing it. Focus on having a sense of control over the transition. Use your triggers and symbolic images every time you perform the transition until it becomes effortless!

Try this: Use Imagery To Control Your Anger

Some skaters get triggered by situations they perceive as negative such as being blocked illegally. These situations may make the skater angry and this emotion takes away their ability to perform at their best by distracting them from their most appropriate focus and limiting their ability to make effective decisions.

A skater can use imagery to picture their trigger situations happening, practice refocusing, see themselves redirecting the anger in a productive way and performing well after the negative event. Practicing the desired response through imagery will help the skater to be able to make this a reality.

Imagine skater A is playing in a game and an opposing skater B flails her arms, smacking skater A in the face. Skater A's typical reaction is to feel offended by skater B's actions, thinking she should not have done it. Skater A would typically follow up those thoughts by screaming at skater B something like, "Watch your hands, bitch!" and then trying to get some revenge hits on her. Some negative consequences of this action have been skater A getting distracted and missing the opposing jammer's return to the pack or going to the penalty box for cussing.

Here is an example of an imagery script skater A could use to practice her desired response to this situation. The skater would start by picturing the trigger event:

Deep breath in…breathe out…let the anger swell up from the bottom of your skates, into your legs, all the way through your core and chest. Feel the anger flowing down out of your arms, feel the hot emotions bursting out your fingers. Squeeze all of that anger into your fists. Take a deep breath. Relax your hands. Breathe out and think, *She is not my focus, where is their jammer?* Look for her. Get ready for the attack. Put all of your anger into your hunt.

Using Imagery to Energize

There are certain times during a game when we could use a pick-me-up in energy. Picturing yourself as a machine, animal or force of nature can help you be able to create energy at will. This strategy is particularly useful when you may begin to feel fatigued such as towards the end of a particularly physical game or during a tournament, when a point spread starts to widen or when a sudden burst of energy is needed to finish a play. You can even have different energizing cues to call upon during different game situations.

Some examples of energizing cues are:

Freight Train	*Fighter jet*	*Springing Cobra*
Gazelle	*Charging Bull*	*Beast Unleashed*
Tornado	*Lightning*	*Can of Whoop-Ass*

Here is a scenario where a jammer might utilize imagery to energize herself: It is a minute into a jam and there are no lead jammers. The opposing jammer has just gone to the box creating a power jam situation. The jammer in our example, has already been knocked around quite a bit and is feeling it. Her team has already had a series of unsuccessful star passes so the jammer is hesitant to risk it. They are down in points and this is a big opportunity. She needs every bit of energy she can gather to deal with the opposing team's tough defense. On the approach to the pack the jammer will combine imagery with self-talk and focusing. She will let go of all other thoughts except for those that are helpful in this moment. Her energizing cue is a tank, which for her represents strength, invincibility and intimidation. She will visualize herself as this huge machine, made of metal, menacing and indestructible. She will imagine that she, as the tank, is charging at speed towards the opposing blockers. She will think, *I am a tank. Unstoppable. Forward, forward, forward. Strong.*

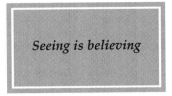

Seeing is believing

Plan for when you will use your energizing cues ahead of time and practice them. You will want to find places in the game where there is a lapse in action. Sitting on the bench waiting to go out on the next jam, those few seconds before a jam starts or the time a jammer has while lapping around to the pack are all great moments to utilize for energy management.

"I kind of close my eyes and I kind of picture myself in a pack. I imagine I'm a blocker and I'm just the strongest going out there and hitting the hardest. Obviously there are girls out there that hit harder than me but this is how I see myself. I tell myself you're ready for this, you can do this. Be here, be strong." — EMTease, age 33, skating 5 years

Using Imagery To Practice While Injured

Because imagery allows skaters to practice their mental toughness skills, strategies and technical skills without ever having to lace up their skates, it is the ideal way to be able to continue to train while out on an injury. You can go over practice drills, work on plays, develop strategies — everything! Mental practice sends the same messages between your brain and body that physical practice does. So, using this technique will speed your ability to get back into the swing of things when you return. Things won't seem as unfamiliar and the relearning curve won't be so steep.

Try this: Use Imagery To Prepare For Any Situation

Hostile crowds, unexpected game situations, getting blown away in points, being close to fouling out, bright lights, unsporting conduct from opposing players and more. What are your game stressors? You can use imagery to mentally prepare for any situation. When using this technique, see yourself responding to the situation in the best way possible, not necessarily how you've responded in the past.

Try this: Image Yourself As Your Hero!

Most derby girls out there are going to have a superstar skater they look up to and admire. Find some video clips of your heroine skating in games. While watching the videos imagine that you *are* the skater. Feel her movements in your body as if you are making them. Feel the impact of hits. What does it feel like to go that fast? Feel the muscles that she is using. What do things look like through her eyes? Feel how her skates are balanced underneath her, the edges that she is riding on. Feel how her weight is shifting and so on.

Next close your eyes and imagine yourself doing some of the moves you witnessed. Imagine this as accurately as possible, using as many of your senses as possible. This exercise allows newer skaters to experience and grow to a higher level of skating.

Learning to use imagery takes practice. As with physical skating practice, trying it sporadically or occasionally is not going to be very effective. It takes regular practice in order to get skilled enough to make it really worthwhile. But once you get it, imagery will be an invaluable tool that can help you bridge the gap between where you are and where you want to be.

"My focus right now is just speed. I'm so ungodly slow. I watch (my super fast teammate) and see how she does it and what makes her so fast." — Paisley, age 21, fresh meat

4 wheels move the body,

8 wheels move the soul

10

WIN WITH GRACE, LOSE WITH CLASS

Roller derby is a competitive sport. The main way we measure whether one team is better than another is by the results on the scoreboard. However, it is important to keep the concept of winning and losing in perspective. Wins and losses are not absolute values.

When does winning mean the most?

- when you beat a team that is equal to or better than your team

- when your team plays their best

When is a win not as significant?

- when you beat a weaker team

- when you played dirty to win

When is a loss the most devastating?

- when you didn't play your best

- when you lose against a team that isn't as good as your team

When is losing not so bad?

- when you lose to a better team

- when your team plays its best to the very last whistle

"Losing isn't so bad when you get MVP."

—Wombpunch, age 26, skating 4 years

Performance, Process And Outcome Goals

Recall from Chapter 3, goals in sports can be divided into three distinct categories: performance, process and outcome goals. Performance and process goals are goals that you can achieve independent of your opponent. That means these are things that you have control over. In Chapter 6, you learned that we don't have control over what others do, but we can control our own actions. Setting performance and process goals ensures a team has a chance of being successful no matter what the scoreboard says at the end of the game. Performance goals are those that you set in relation to your own past performance. Some examples of performance goals are:

- Stay out of the box the entire first half

- Attempt a star pass

- Re-enter correctly to avoid track cutting penalties

- Always know when the opposing jammer is coming (no surprises!)

- Give one assist per jam

Process goals are the actions that you need to perform well. This is breaking down being a good derby player into bite size pieces that add up to high level skills. Some examples of process goals are:

- Keep my eye on the opposing jammer

- Exhale when making a hit

- Keep my knees bent

Outcome goals focus on end results such as winning. Outcome goals have been shown to be less effective than performance and process goals in helping an athlete to reach their optimal level of play. Outcome goals may depend on the actions of others which are not under our control. Setting goals which are only partially under our control sets us up for becoming frustrated with the goal setting process. Despite a superior effort, your outcome goal may not be achieved. Focusing on outcome goals may also usurp the inherent pleasure of the game because it causes skaters to be overly focused on the ends and not relish in the means. Teams and individual skaters should have performance and process goals going in to a game as well as outcome goals. Some examples of outcome goals for both individual skaters and teams are:

- Win the game

- Be the fastest skater on the team

- Always get lead jammer

- Score 25 points in one jam

- Make it into the championships

Focusing on performance and process goals give you a better sense of control and this will build confidence. Overemphasizing outcome goals can cause anxiety, especially on game day. Outcome goals are great for increasing motivation at practice and helping a skater and team develop long term goals. However, on game day set clear performance and process goals. The really cool thing is, the more a skater or a team focuses on performance and process goals the more games they will end up winning! Determining what you focus on during a game can affect your performance and your enjoyment of the sport.

It Can Be Lonely At the Top

A derby skater enters into the sport with different levels of skill. Some have extensive skating knowledge from speed skating, figure skating, hockey or other experiences. Others have never skated in their life. However, almost every skater has the goal of improving and may have role models in derby that they look up to and admire and think, *I want to be just like them when I grow up.* The great thing about derby is that if you stick with it, set goals and push yourself you will improve. It won't be long before you may find yourself in the position of being one of the best on your team or your region or even the world.

Skaters who are at the top of the heap may find they feel a mixed bag of emotions in this position. On the one hand, they are incredibly proud of their accomplishments. And they should be. They worked insanely hard to get where they are. They receive attention, accolades and lots of playing time. On the other hand, they may experience a ton of pressure in holding and maintaining this position. They may also feel it is their responsibility to make sure their team wins. If she happens to have an off day and her team ends up losing, a top skater may think it is her fault and she has let her team down. Also, top skaters may feel the pressure from the up-and-comers nipping at their heels. As the saying goes, once you are at the top there is nowhere to go but down.

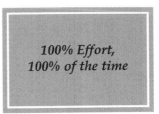

100% Effort,
100% of the time

Some skaters may deal with all these pressures by avoiding the top position all together. They may not perform their absolute best at practices and games, preferring to remain a "B" student, which is good but keeps them out of the spotlight. A top skater needs to talk to their coach and teammates about any internal struggles they are experiencing. Keeping an open dialogue will help ensure that they are able to give 100% and not let being awesome become detrimental.

"It is one thing to be declared the winner, it is quite another to really win."

— Josephson Institute (2014)

Getting Your Ass Kicked: The Ultimate Compliment.

Two of the toughest times to give 100% is when you are clearly winning and clearly losing. The team that is ahead may start adjusting their game to what the other team is bringing rather than playing at their full potential. The winning team may start delivering just enough muscle to get the job done and keep the lead, rather than giving it everything possible. Some may see this as being merciful or creating an even game that is more enjoyable to the fans. But that is not authentic roller derby. What is the message that you are giving the other team when you sandbag? That you feel sorry for them? That you don't think they can handle it? That they are so weak you barely need to give any effort to pull off a win? Show the other team that they are worthy of your very best and don't pull your punches. Let the point spread on the scoreboard be truly representative of the difference between the two teams. Sometimes an ass kicking is the ultimate compliment.

There are other ways besides sandbagging that a winning team can utilize to continue to play their best while acknowledging they have a sizable lead and more skill level. Is there a new play that you've been dying to try out? With an extensive lead it is a great opportunity to give it a shot. Are there skaters on your team that don't usually get a lot of playing time? Send them out on the track as a unit with instructions to maintain the lead and not give up any points. No matter who is out on the track they need to give it absolutely everything they've got. This is why you're here.

And for the losing team? Going up against a better team than yours shows guts. If you are able to stay focused and continue to play at your best without giving up that shows the world that you deserve to be there — on the track with the top teams. Look for the positives to make every game valuable. For example, what better way to learn some crazy, new maneuvers than by experiencing them being used against you?

> *"The arrogance of some skaters when you start to lose and you get that show pony attitude of the allstars of the team. They kind of take the reins. It becomes no longer a team, it's a one-man-show. It's discouraging because you have teammates who are trying but then you have the talking down to you and kind of emotionally beating you up and your self-esteem. Frustrations come out. It brings the mood down and it was a bad loss."* — EMTease, age 33, skating 5 years

Win As A Team, Lose As A Team

Ensure everyone on the team, even skaters who are not playing due to injury or not making the cut, feels like they have ownership in the team's wins and losses. This will build your bonds as a strong team. If you didn't play don't tell your friends, "Wow, they did great out there." Instead say, "Wow, we did really great tonight." Conversely, if you didn't play and your team lost you could say "We had a tough night" rather than "They had a tough night." This is the way superfans talk about their favorite teams. They discuss their team's performance in terms of *us* and *we* rather than *they*. This is because superfans feel an emotional connection to their teams and feel personally affected by what happens to them. By simply changing your wording you can enhance your ownership in your team.

Another way for everyone on the team to own wins and losses is to assign roles to everyone, including those injured or not rostered. Injured skaters can be scouts and watch the opposing team for strategies, plays or skaters that are making an impact on your team. They can then report this information at halftime, being involved in the team's halftime meeting. Non-rostered skaters can watch your team to look for things your skaters are doing well and provide positive feedback and encouragement to the team at halftime. You can also have announcers call out the whole team's names, not just those who are skating, and have everyone listed in the program.

"Winning is really, really fun. But as long as you learn from your loss and improve next time, losing isn't the biggest thing that ever happened."

— Punching Judy, age 47, skating 10 years

Attributions

In sports psychology attributions are the explanations an athlete gives for the outcome of their performance. An attribution can be either negative or positive. An individual will tend to use mainly negative or positive attributions to explain their wins or losses. Using negative attributions to describe reasons for winning or losing decreases confidence and gives you expectations of failure in the future. Using positive attributions enhances your confidence, gives you expectations of success in the future and ultimately will improve your performance. Here are some different types of attributions (Etnier, 2009):

> *How you handle a loss is part of what defines you as a person.*

Missed opportunity. This is a negative attribution for a win. A missed opportunity occurs when you have a great game and don't take credit for it. For example, you have just blocked like a brick house the whole game and no jammers got by you without first experiencing some serious pain. After the game a friend says, "You did amazing out there! How do you do it?" Imagine you respond by saying, "Their jammers weren't very tough. I got lucky a lot of the time. Most of it was due to my teammates helping me." This may seem like the polite, modest response but it doesn't give you any credit. You have just missed an opportunity for confidence building!

Taking credit. This is a positive attribution for a win. Don't forget about all the training, effort and skill that contributed to your performance. It is okay to say, "Thanks! I have been really preparing for this game and I tried focusing on making really hard hits tonight." This statement gives you credit for your part in your performance. When you take credit you build your self-confidence.

Taking the blame. This occurs when an athlete takes all of the blame for their team's loss. This negative attribution typically occurs when the loss occurs in the final seconds of the game. For example, a team is up by 10 points and their jammer goes to the box in the last jam giving the opposing jammer the opportunity to score 15 points and win the game by 5 points. A skater may blame themselves, saying, *I lost the game for my team.* The reason taking the blame for this kind of loss is inaccurate is there were many other factors that went into the final score. Throughout the game there were lots of other jams with opportunities for scoring, defending, making strategic decisions, and so on, that led to the score being so close at the end. A team must be sure not to put undue blame on a skater in this position following a loss. Make sure your team owns all wins and losses together, as a team.

Poor process. This is a positive attribution for a loss. Instead of the jammer in the example above saying the loss was due to her being a sucky jammer, she will instead attribute her trip to the box to poor performance processes such as failing to enter into the pack correctly after getting knocked out or using her forearms to push off of an opponent. By explaining the mistake in terms of things she can work on rather than her just being a terrible jammer, she can continue to set goals to improve and protect her confidence. This is much more positive than declaring herself the worst jammer on the planet who should never be allowed to wear the star again.

Another negative attribution for a loss is **blaming others.** This occurs when you blame the loss on dirty play by the opponents, bad ref calls or your teammates. Blaming others may protect you from having to take an honest look at your own weaknesses, which can be painful. But blaming others does not give you the opportunity for learning and growth because none of the elements you pinpointed are within your control to change.

"I never go into a game thinking I'm going to lose."

— Wombpunch, age 26, skating 4 years

Try this: Blame Pie-Chart

If you struggle with blaming yourself or others for losses this activity can help you to begin to see situations in a more realistic and balanced way. Think of a recent game your team lost. Draw a circle and then "slice" pieces of the pie to serve up blame to those you feel deserve it. When you are done look to see if you are eating too much of the blame yourself or are giving too much to others. If the entire pie is yours or others there may be some

 inaccuracies in your perceptions. Look to see which of the slices are things that you can use as lessons to improve your or your team's performance for the next game. Those elements are the ones that you want to focus on. As long as you are always learning, a loss is partly a win. Check out the example of a completed Blame-Pie Chart (Figure 10.1).

Figure 10.1 Blame Pie-Chart Example

Develop A Healthy Attitude Towards Competition

Weinberg and Gould (2011) describe *achievement motivation* as referring to the drive that an individual has to excel, to achieve their goals, to push past obstacles and to strive for success when being compared with others or with their own past performance. In sports, achievement motivation is often called competiveness. A skater's state of competiveness will affect many of their thoughts, feelings and actions. To see how your achievement motivation influences you, answer the following questions:

- Do you seek out opponents with equal ability to yourself or do you prefer going up against skaters of much greater or lesser skill?

- How do you perform when being evaluated?

- How much effort to you put in to achieving your derby goals? How often do you go to practice or train outside of practice?

- How hard do you try at practice? At how many practices do you take it easy versus giving it everything you've got?

- When you face failure or things get tough do you try harder or back off your efforts?

- Are you more motivated by achieving success or by avoiding failure?

- Do you attribute successes to things that are within your control? How about failures?

A skater with high achievement motivation will have an easy time playing their best and will have the most fun during a tight race that is anyone's game. A skater with low achievement motivation will seek out opponents of much greater ability or much lesser ability so their win or loss will be guaranteed. For them, losing to an evenly matched opponent would be distressing. High achievers seek out difficult challenges and prefer intermediate risks.

High achievers perform well when being evaluated. They think about the possibility of doing well and will look for situations where they can show what they can do. Low achievers perform worse when they are being evaluated. They are consumed by fears of failure and will avoid taking risks.

A skater with high achievement motivation will put in a lot of work to pursue their goals. They will attend as many practices as possible and put in an intense level of effort. A skater with low achievement motivation won't put a lot of work towards accomplishing their goals and when the going gets tough will put forward even less work. High achievers will increase their determination in the face of adversity.

High achievers are motivated by achieving success while low achievers are motivated by wanting to avoid failure. High achievers will attribute success to things within their control (effort) and failure to things outside their control (tough opponent). Low achievers will attribute success to things outside their control (good reffing) and failure to things within their control (bad game strategy).

So how does one develop high achievement motivation?

Assess your attributional style. If you notice yourself making negative attributions, change them to positive ones. Explain successes using internal factors within your control. Explain failures using external factors outside your control.

Consider your personality. If you are motivated by avoiding failure, push yourself to accept challenges where there is a 50/50 chance of losing. Expose yourself to situations where you will be evaluated.

Decide when competition is appropriate. There are times to compete against others and there are times when you should focus on your own individual improvement.

Downplay outcome goals. Concentrate instead on mastering skills.

"I love a really tight game. I love a hard fought game over a blow out any day."

— Punching Judy, age 47, skating 10 years

Win With Class, Lose With Grace

A very important mental toughness skill is the ability to tolerate a loss. Every game, win or lose, should be turned into a learning experience that ultimately improves a skater's and a team's performance. Being able to see losses as necessary components on the path to excellence will help an athlete to be able to handle failure. It is helpful to remember that those who experience the fewest losses are those that never make it because they end up quitting.

Jerry Lynch, proposes ways to think about losing that will help an athlete to be able to tolerate it better (2001, p. 191):

- "All physical skills, no matter how difficult, are always perfected through mistakes and failures, by falling and getting up, again and again.

- All great athletes identify what they have learned in defeat and begin to see how it helps them to higher levels.

- Ups and downs are natural; you win some, you lose some.

- It is healthy to take ourselves less seriously.

- Failure is not devastating. Disappointing, yes!

- You can't avoid failure. There are only two kinds of athletes: those who fail, and those who will. So begin to see its value."

Lynch also suggests expanding the traditional definition of winning to include victories of the heart and mind that can help make losses on the scoreboard less painful. Inner triumphs can include overcoming self-doubt, fear and ego and accomplishments such as pushing your body to its limits and reaching your potential. What are the characteristics of a champion? Choosing to be fearless, relaxed, fluid, prepared, passionate or tenacious can empower you by giving you behaviors to focus on

> "The arrow that hits the bull's-eye is the result of a hundred misses."
>
> —Jerry Lynch, Creative Coaching (2001)

that you can control. Concentrating on personal ways to win that are separate from the scoreboard can make every single game highly valuable and satisfying.

If someone who didn't know if you had won or lost looked at photographs of your team after the game would they be able to tell what the results were? Make sure to maintain good sporting behavior even after the game has ended by smiling, slapping the other team's hands and congratulating them on their win. Act the same whether you have won or lost!

Be careful not to diminish the other team's win by telling them a bunch of excuses as to why you didn't win, even if they are legitimate. When you tell your opponents things like, *Our best skaters weren't playing because they were out with injuries* or *Five of our skaters were playing with the flu* you are giving the other team the message that they did not deserve to win or that their win didn't mean that much. If you feel your team could have played a better game, get your stuff together, schedule a rematch and bring it! But for now, let your opponents have their time in the sun.

Try this: Separating Our Identity From Our Results

Your self-worth and identity should not be based on the results of your derby performance. In the circles in Figure 10.3, write words that describe you: the roles you play, interests you have and so on. "Derby" can only be in one of the circles! Add more circle if needed. Next draw a big circle around all the little circles. The larger circle represents the total picture of who you are. Then obliterate the circle that says "derby." You can do this by scribbling it out, drawing little knives stabbing it, covering it with a sticker...whatever. Get creative. This represents having a really crappy game or other derby failure. Notice that there are many other areas of your life that can't be affected by a poor derby performance. Finding balance in our lives helps reduce the pressure from competing. A bad performance only affects a very small part of who we are. Figure 10.2 shows an example.

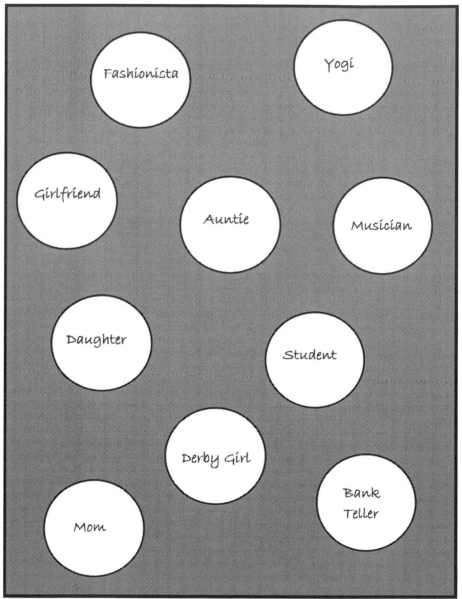

Figure 10.2 Separating Our Identity From Our Results Example

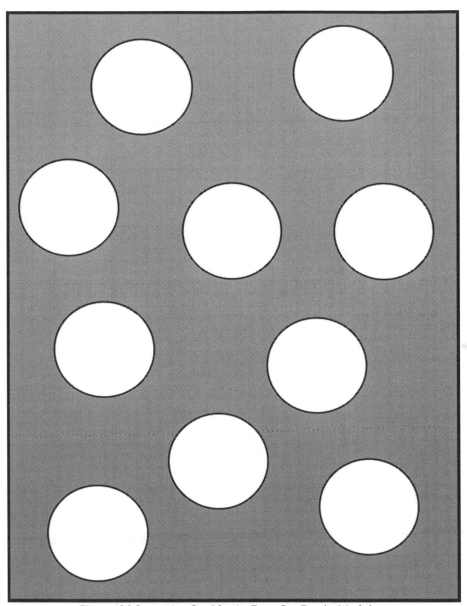

Figure 10.3 Separating Our Identity From Our Results Worksheet

Try this: Define What Is Necessary To Play Like A Champion.

Focusing on how you are performing in a game rather than whether you are winning helps you to hold on to your confidence. Jerry Lynch (2001) suggests coming up with four traits, behaviors or actions that define championship level play and then committing to them with a signed contract similar to the one below. For example, a champion derby skater will jump on every opportunity to make an assist, will always know where the opposing jammer is, will make hard hits and never give up regardless of the score. Commit to play like a champion individually or as a team by reading the contract aloud to each other.

> *"We won. But what made it so good was we were the underdogs. We had 95% new girls and it was really nice and cohesive and there was a lot of communication between the veterans and the newer girls. We wanted to win but we did not expect to because we had so many new girls and everybody saw the odds stacked against us."*
>
> *— EMTease, age 33, skating 5 years*

Commitment to Play Like a Champion

I, _____ (skater name) commit to playing like a champion for my team, _____ (team name).

I commit to:

1.

2.

3.

4.

Signed,

_____

11

GET BACK IN THE GAME AFTER AN INJURY

"Injuries happen, I just hope it doesn't happen to me."

— Pinktastic, age 31, fresh meat

Just because an athlete has been medically cleared to return to skating doesn't ensure they are psychologically ready. Emotional recovery is just as important to consider as physical recovery. Some skaters return to competing following an injury confidently and without any worries. For others, however, returning to play following a major injury can create unmanageable stress. Despite being medically cleared, some skaters are just not mentally ready to return. They may be plagued by fears of further injury and haunted by disastrous images of the original incident. This chapter focuses on the psychology of being injured and what skaters can do to help them return to competition following a serious injury.

A skater can experience many of the following after an injury:

Guilt	Anger
Frustration	Doubts
Separation and Loneliness	Hopelessness
Fear and Anxiety	Nightmares
Identity Loss	Lack of Confidence

"I was surprised by how much hurting broke me down. I got in the mindset that I couldn't do things that I could before. I got sad and gave up."

— Paisley, age 21, fresh meat

How a skater responds to an injury is determined more by how they interpret or perceive the injury than by the injury itself. Many factors can influence a skater's perception of the injury. Has the skater experienced an injury before? If not, they may be more stressed as this is new territory. Does the injury impact the skater's job or the ability to care for her family? The further reaching its effects, the more the skater will experience the injury as a loss or threat. How much of an investment does the skater have in roller derby? For those who have achieved success and are intensely involved, the whole focus of their identity, their sense of who they are as people, may be tied up in the role of athlete. For those, an injury can feel devastating. When a skater loses the ability to do the one thing that gave her confidence, she can lose motivation in the other aspects of her life.

How Coaches React Is Important

Ditch old-school attitudes. The way coaches respond to an injured skater can affect the skater's recuperation. Old-school attitudes about toughness in sports (always give 110% and act tough) can cause injury and failure when taken to extremes. Many highly driven derby girls learn to withstand any amount or kind of pain. This makes for a tough skater, but can also make for an often injured skater who never plays in a fully healthy state. This can lead to a short lived career and a lifetime of pain.

Involve injured skaters. Coaches must also avoid giving skaters the message that they are only valuable when they are able to play. Injured skaters should not be isolated from healthy skaters at practices or games.

Forget the guilt trip. Skaters should not be made to feel guilty for not helping their team to win. They should not be made to feel ashamed of being injured or that injuries are something to hide. You should not feel pressured by your coaches to return before you are medically and psychologically ready.

Validate emotions. Coaches should allow skaters the normal expression of feelings that go along with being injured. Coaches should avoid telling skaters to "cheer up" or "suck it up". Grieving is an important and necessary part of the recovery process.

Whole-person philosophy. Coaches and teammates should avoid treating the skater as the injury. You are just as much of an athlete, just as much of a person, as before the injury.

Teammates, Friends And Family Can Also Affect Recovery

Injuries aren't contagious. Teammates may stay away from the injured skater because they represent a threat of injury to themselves. Your teammates may think, *If it can happen to her, it can happen to me.* This can be more of a problem if an injury is particularly gruesome or visible.

Be aware of internal conflict. The injury of one skater may present another skater on her team the opportunity to shine. Your teammates may have mixed feelings when giving you emotional support and wishes for a speedy return. Some level of competition is necessary and healthy within a team, however, it should not ever become personal. Being aware of these potential problems and keeping the lines of communication open can prevent an unfavorable situation.

Continue to socialize. The stronger the skater's identification as an athlete, the more her friends and family may have come to interact with her primarily through her role as an athlete. People may not know quite how to relate to you now. They may only know how to deal with you through your past glory or your future return to skating, not the injured present.

> *Skaters are taught to be invincible. This can lead them to being extremely vulnerable and totally unprepared for an incapacitating injury.*

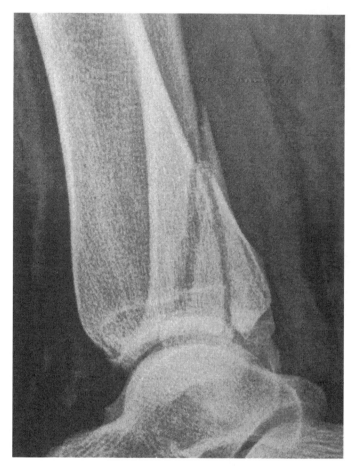

"I broke both my fib and my tib vertically up from my ankle, fractured my talus and endured some soft tissue damage. I've been off skates for 9 months. At this point and time I'm still not able to skate because I can't push off with a horizontal stride, side to side, typical skating motion. I would like to get back to at least skating with my family and with the team in an assistant coach role. I don't know if I'll be back to bouting level or not because one of my bones is not healing."

— OC Triple D, age 35, injured one week prior to what would have been her first game

Factors That Predispose Athletes To Injury

The stress-injury model (Williams, 2006) proposes stressed athletes are more prone to injury. According to this model, those with a history of many stressors, personality characteristics that intensify the stress response and few coping skills to deal with stress will be more likely to see situations such as a demanding practice or crucial game as stressful. The severity of the athlete's stress response is what predisposes them to injury. This model does not mean to blame a skater for their injury, but help her to understand how to reduce the possibility of incurring an injury. The three main culprits of the stress response that lead to injury are 1) muscle tension, 2) narrowed field of awareness and 3) increased distractibility.

History of stressors in an athlete's life include:

- Life change events

- Daily hassles

- Previous injury

Personality characteristics that increase an athlete's risk of injury include:

- Type A behavior: Driven, impatient, high stress personalities

- High anger directed outward, but not inward

- Assertiveness, independence, self-assurance

- External locus of control: A person feels their lives are not under their personal control

- Competitive anxiety: Fears or worries about performances, being evaluated by others, etc.

- Somatic anxiety (experiences anxiety traits in the body like muscle tension or stomach aches)

An athlete's coping resources include:

- Social supports

- Confidence

- Staying focused under pressure

- Being able to self-regulate energy

You can use the many stress interventions included in this book including cognitive reframing, breathing techniques, self-talk and imagery to battle stress and decrease your risk of injury.

What Can Help You To Come Back After An Injury?

Be confident. A skater who is stressed and lacks confidence when she returns to competition will actually be more prone to re-injury. It creates a self-fulfilling prophecy. If you think you will get hurt, you probably will. The fear of injury produces timidity and cautiousness. You won't be participating with the intensity that the circumstances demand. If your head is not 100% in the game then you are more likely to be injured. Use self-talk to tell yourself things like, *I'm strong, I'm safe, I can do this.* Focus on what is going right, rather than on what could go wrong.

Get back to practice! You should rejoin the team as soon as humanly possible, even on crutches or bandaged. When you are away from your team for a length of time you may feel that your team has moved on without you. There may be new jokes, new team members and so on. By being there, you will grow and develop along with your team. Find ways to be involved. For example, you can follow a teammate who plays a similar position and give feedback while mentally engaging in the drills and skills.

Use a peer mentor. Talk to a skater who has successfully rehabilitated and returned from an injury. They can give you tips and suggestions from a firsthand point of view.

Separate pain from injury. Learn to differentiate between pain and injury, pressure and damage. Some amount of "playing through pain" is a normal part of muscle exertion. But some kinds of pain should not be ignored. Along with this, skaters should learn what the appropriate amount of pain is that one should tolerate.

Look for the silver lining. It can be helpful to develop positive meaning from the injury. Not in a lame, fake way, but in a genuine, personal growth kind of way. For example, some injured athletes have come out of injuries with better/smarter technical skating, increased mental toughness and clearer priorities. Being injured and recovering, living through it, can teach us that we are stronger than we thought we were. It can show us how much we can endure. Living through an injury can reduce fear of future injuries because we know that we are strong and can heal. It can also give us more drive to excel in derby because we realize we might not have a chance to do this again.

> *"I got a high ankle sprain, which is worse than a break or a regular sprain as this injury shifts bones and pulls several ligaments. If effects the foot, ankle, lower leg bones, and knee. I am expected to fully return 100%. This injury was by far the worst because, after all, derby, or so I thought, was my only source of happiness! Silver lining by friend, silver lining."* — Loogie Vuitton, age 32, skating 6 years

Be sad. Understand reasonable responses to an injury. Grieving is a normal and necessary part of getting over anything sucky in life. It's normal to feel frustrated and disappointed. It's normal to feel angry or to wish it hadn't happened. It's not reasonable to feel hopeless, worthless, that the injury is a sign of weakness or that your life is over. If your normal responses to injury don't fade in time or if you are experiencing extreme responses, seek help.

Be informed. Learn about the injury itself and the rehabilitation process. Lacking knowledge can increase anxiety. Being informed can help you to become an active participant in the process.

> *"The pain that I experienced this go round was just ridonculous. I had two children and I had a C-section on both and this was right up there with that pain. Hurt was an understatement."* — EMTease, age 33, skating 5 years

View rehab as an athletic challenge. It can help to get through rehabilitation if you conceptualizes it as an athletic challenge that should be taken on with the same intensity and precision that you put into your skating routine.

Use imagery. Visualize returning to competition and kicking butt. We tend to imagine the worst that could happen. Instead, imagine situations that bring on feelings of pride, accomplishment, enthusiasm and confidence. If visualization is difficult for you, look at videos or photos of yourself making an awesome block or juking around that last line of defense.

Set goals. Collaborate with your coaches on short and long term goals. For example, "I will skate 10 laps today," "By the end of the month I will scrimmage in three jams," and "I will skate in our July game." Make goals measurable, attainable and realistic. Goal setting will increase your commitment to fully returning to competing. As you accomplish goals you will feel successful and your confidence will grow. Be sure to push yourself a little bit out of your comfort zone each practice to ensure you make progress and don't stagnate.

Practice relaxation. Playing while rigid or anticipating pain or injury is dangerous and will lead to re-injury. Also, tensions in the injured area can increase pain and work against the effectiveness of rehabilitation.

Ultimately, the decision to continue to skate following an injury is each individual's personal decision. Every skater has to do their own cost/benefit analysis. Is what you get out of playing roller derby worth the risk of further injury? Whether it's the thrill of competition, the fitness, the rollergirl status, whatever… those who go back decide that the payoff is worth it for *them*.

> *"I've broken my ankle twice. The second time I broke it, I broke my weight bearing bone. I had to stay off skates for a while. I had a boot on and I had to be cleared to skate but then I got right back on skates (and was bouting two months later). I've seen a lot of girls break things and be afraid to get back out there. It's a mental block and I didn't want to do that. It probably wasn't the smartest decision I ever made but I didn't want to be afraid to get back out there. So I started very slowly at practice. I just went back out there and said, 'You know what? You're going to do this because if you don't you're going to think about it and you're going to get scared and you're not going to do it.' Because I'm not young, I'm not 18."* — Punching Judy, age 47, skating 10 years

148

12

BEING A GOOD SPORT

"We're all here for the same goal."

— Paisley. Age 21, fresh meat

Roller derby provides the perfect environment for challenging yourself to build the mental toughness skill of sportsmanship. Spending a lot of time with the same group of people in competitive, adrenaline charged settings can bring out the worst in some. Instead, see the derby environment as an opportunity to bring out the best in you. Don't settle for only working on your strength, speed and technical skills. Work to develop your personal character alongside your physical skills. Growth in character can be the best derby souvenir of all.

"I like it when the other team's laughing and able to have a conversation with you in between jams."

— Wombpunch, age 26, skating 4 years

What Does It Mean To Be A Good Sport?

While there isn't a single definition of what being a good sport or sportsmanship means, it has to do with what we believe is the right and wrong way to act in sports — sports morality. When used in sports psychology, the term *moral* does not imply religious values.

Many sports organizations have codes of conduct to guide athletes as to how they are expected to act. However, they may be in general terms that skaters have a hard time translating into specific actions. The Women's Flat Track Derby Association's Code of Conduct includes the words, "individuals should display sports like behavior and abide by the rules, regulations, policies and procedures and laws of all corresponding agencies," "display good judgment," and "treat one another with respect dignity and fairness." USA Roller Sports' Code of Conduct includes the following:

1. I will not engage in unsportsmanlike conduct with any coach, player, participant, official or any other attendee.

2. I will not encourage my child, or any other person, to engage in unsportsmanlike conduct with any coach, parent, player, participant, official or any other attendee.

3. I will not engage in any behavior which would endanger the health, safety or well-being of any coach, player, participant, official or any other attendee.

4. I will not encourage any other person to engage in any behavior which would endanger the health, safety or well-being of any coach, player, participant, official or any other attendee.

5. I will not use drugs or alcohol while participating in a sport event.

6. I will not encourage any other person to use drugs or alcohol while participating in a sport event.

7. I will treat any coach, player, participant, official or any other attendee with respect regardless of race, creed, color, national origin, sex, sexual orientation or ability.

8. I will not engage in verbal or physical threats or abuse aimed at any coach, player, participant, official or any other attendee.

9. I will not encourage any other person to engage in verbal or physical threats or abuse aimed at any coach, parent, player, participant, official or any other attendee.

10. I will not initiate a fight or scuffle with any coach, player, participant, official of any other attendee.

11. I will not encourage any other person to initiate a fight or scuffle with any coach, parent, player, participant, official or any other attendee.

Additionally, most leagues also have their own codes of conduct that skaters agree to follow when they join the league. Here are some ways to break down the general term, *sportsmanship*, into specific actions that each skater can do:

- Watch your tone of voice when talking to the refs.
- Smile and shake or slap hands with opponents after a game, regardless of whether you won or lost.
- Acknowledge that an opponent did a good job.
- Respect your coach and captains.
- Lend equipment to an opponent if they need something.
- Refuse to take advantage of injured opponents.
- During a scrimmage, admit you committed a penalty that nobody saw.
- Keep your cool after making a mistake.
- Know your own limits and avoid endangering others.
- Don't trash talk other teams.
- Give a downed opponent a hand up after the jam has ended.
- Shake hands with the referees and thank them after the game.
- Show up and work hard at practices.
- Acknowledge mistakes and try to improve.
- Make only positive comments to spectators.
- Be happy for a teammate's success rather feeling negative emotions like jealousy or even hatred.
- Don't blame others for your bad behavior. Be accountable!
- Don't celebrate your opponents' failures.

In essence, being a good sport means winning comes second to fair play when the two come into conflict. Skaters learn from their role models, so coaches need to be sure to demonstrate good sporting behavior as well. When a coach has a bad reaction to a questionable ref call but expects their skaters to be able to handle it, that doesn't work so well. Coaches should model for their skaters how they expect them to act. Coaches need to lose the *Do as I say, not as I do* attitude.

> *"You have to respect everybody that officiates the game, that plays in the game, that helps,…the NSO's… You have to because it's a contact sport and otherwise you're going to get hurt. When girls don't respect that is when girls get really injured. So you have to have sportsmanship out there."*
>
> *– Punching Judy, age 47, skating 10 years.*

Levels Of Moral Reasoning In Sports

Sports psychologists have developed five different levels of moral reasoning that an athlete will progress through. As an athlete's moral reasoning develops, their decisions go from being made from a self – centered perspective to what is in the best interest of all involved. Not everyone will reach Level 5 and even if you are capable of a high level of moral decision making you may not use it. Often we may be using several different levels simultaneously.

Level 1: Decisions about what is right and wrong are made based on whether or not one can get away with it and what the outcome is. When using this level of reasoning a skater would decide it is okay to kick the skates of her opponents if she can get away with it and it is an effective strategy.

Level 2: This is the "give what you get" stage. An athlete may decide something is right because somebody else did it to them. For example, a skater would make the decision to start grabbing and pushing an opposing skater because it was done to her the whole first half.

Level 3: At this level an athlete treats others as they want to be treated. Such as, a skater would decide she does not like to be cussed at and would take care not to cuss at other skaters.

Level 4: Decisions about what is right or wrong are based on rules and regulations. Using this level of reasoning, a skater would not elbow an opposing skater even if she had an opportunity to do so without penalty.

Level 5: At this level decisions are made based on what is best for all parties involved, regardless of the rules and regulations. For example, even

152

though it is allowed by the rules a skater might decide not to target an opposing skater who they know has a knee injury.

When it comes to translating moral reasoning into action, a skater's decisions will be influenced by factors such as personal psychological resources, the coach's influence, the actions of fans and team norms. Consider the following moral dilemma:

You are the team captain. On your team the captain makes decisions about lineups during competitions. There are less than ten minutes left in the game and your team is ahead by 30 points. One of the skaters on your team has not gotten to play yet because your team was behind for most of the game and you chose to play more experienced skaters. Now that you've taken the lead she asks if she can go in. What would you decide to do?

If you let her skate there is a chance you could lose your lead and not have time to regain it before the end of the game. Your decision about whether or not to let her skate would be made after balancing your moral values with what you as captain might gain or lose and what the team as a whole might gain or lose. Some of the elements that might factor into your decision follow.

Possible outcomes:

- You could play her and win and then everyone would be happy: the fans, your coach, the rest of your team, you and the newer skater.

- You could play her and lose which might satisfy the newer skater but upset others.

Your personal experience:

- You have been in her skates before and know what it feels like to sit on the bench for the whole game when you feel you could contribute.

- In the past, skaters that have not gotten to play in games have quit the team.

- You typically like to give everyone on the team the chance to skate during games when possible, keeping in mind the goal of winning. You try to balance fairness with competitiveness.

Team norms:

- What is your team's philosophy regarding winning or losing vs. fairness to all skaters?

- What has your coach taught you to do in this type of situation?

Personal psychological makeup:

- If you make a decision that is unpopular with the fans and the rest of the team do you have the strength to deal with that?

- How important is integrity to you?

Moral decisions don't have clear right or wrong answers. Solving moral dilemmas means weighing several, often competing or contradictory, factors before arriving at a course of action. Keep in mind, what may be a moral dilemma for one person might be a simple decision for another.

Aggression And Violence

"I don't mind blocking hard but when you're just mean, when you're just point blank illegal to hurt somebody? I don't want to be on the floor with you and I don't want you on my team."
– Punching Judy, age 47, skating 10 years.

With an inherently aggressive sport like roller derby it can be difficult to know where to draw the line between what is needed to play your best and what is going too far. The rules provide one way to determine what is condoned and what is considered excessive violence. But if it were as easy as that, aggression would not be the issue it is in full contact sports. Part of the reason for the controversy is that two people watching the same hit might disagree whether it was acceptable aggression or over the top aggression. It depends on their interpretation. Rather than having a discussion about whether or not aggression is good or bad, this section discusses different aspects of aggression from a neutral standpoint.

From a sports psychology viewpoint, aggression is defined as, "any form of behavior directed toward the goal of harming or injuring another living being who is motivated to avoid such treatment" (Baron & Richardson, 1994, p. 7). This is different from the use of the word aggressive to describe assertive behavior, such as when a coach tells a blocker, "Be aggressive out there!" To qualify as aggressive behavior there has to be an *intent* to harm or injure a person. So if you hurt someone but it was an accident it is not aggression. Kicking a team bench is not aggression because the bench is not a living being. However, if you are trying to kick the bench into someone in order to harm them, that is aggression. Additionally, injury can be either physical or psychological so aggression can come in the form of verbal behavior as well.

Aggression develops through a combination of observation and reinforcement. When an athlete sees others modeling aggressive behavior they will learn to be aggressive. Aggressive behavior will increase if that behavior is rewarded. This could come in the form of recognition from fans, coaches, teammates or others. Reinforcement could also come in the form of being able to intimidate the opposition. If a skater is able to cause some serious pain or terror to an opponent early on in the game then the skater may have an easier time the rest of the game because the opponent may avoid her. If an athlete is punished for aggressive behavior, such as knowing they will be benched for the next game, they may decide to curb their aggression. Feeling guilty can also be a negative consequence for one's actions. If an athlete was intentionally playing outside the rules of the sport and ended up causing serious injury to another person they not play aggressively any more.

Certain situations make it more likely for aggressive behaviors to come out:

- Being provoked
- Losing

- An intense rivalry
- Not playing well

Aggression in sports is divided into two categories. *Hostile aggression* is when the main goal is to harm an opponent. *Instrumental aggression* is when injury to another happens during the pursuit of another goal, such as trying to assist your jammer. Some examples of instrumental aggression are:

- A blocker lands on top of the opposing jammer in a pile-up and digs her elbow into the jammer as she gets up off of her, trying to cause her injury.

- A jammer, about to start a jam, tells the opposing jammer, "You might as well give up and go home right now, you've got nothing," trying to cause psychological discomfort and anxiety which will negatively affect the opposing jammer's performance.

- A coach instructs a less skilled player to commit an aggressive act on a highly skilled opponent with the intention of provoking the superior skater into a fight so she will get ejected from the game.

An example of hostile aggression is the position of *Enforcer* that exists in some full contact sports. This player has the exclusive job of hurting members of the opposite team. This role has also been nicknamed things like Assassin, Thug, Hitman and Security.

Another example of hostile aggression comes from the National Football League (NFL). In 2012, the New Orleans Saints were sanctioned when it was discovered they were paying their players $1500 for knocking someone out of the game and $1000 for getting a player carted off the field. A topic closely related to aggression is *violence*. In sports, violence can refer to the level of physical force involved. The enforcer position and big, heart pounding hits in professional sports continue and are glorified despite fines and sanctions. Steelers linebacker James Harrison has been labeled a "one-man concussion machine" (Solotaroff, 2011). In one game he drilled two different opposing players with helmet to helmet contact, icing them both. Neither hit was flagged and Harrison denied any intent to harm, but the intensity of the hits caused injury and he was labeled a dirty player.

The level of violence in sports such as football and hockey has been increasingly questioned with the awareness that a history of concussions is linked to the development of depression and dementia-related syndromes later in life (Guskiewicz, et al., 2005 & 2007). High profile cases have brought this subject into the public eye. In 2014, nine former professional hockey players filed a lawsuit against the National Hockey League stating the league "intentionally created, fostered and promoted a culture of extreme violence" that valued profit over player safety (Klein & Belson, 2014). In 2012, former San Diego Charger, Junior Seau committed suicide.

It was later found that he had suffered from chronic traumatic encephalopathy, a type of brain damage related to repeated head injuries. In 2013, his family sued the NFL for the brain injuries he suffered during his career.

Aggression and violence in roller derby need to be considered. Aggression has been shown to be related to an increase in athletes being injured over what would happen during normal sports participation (Weinberg & Gould, 2011). This is a concern for our sport and for our best performance because we need skaters to be healthy and skating for both roller derby and ourselves to remain strong. If too many skaters leave the sport due to injury the sport can't sustain itself. If our competition has been annihilated who would our team have to play? If our best opponents are all out on injury, who will motivate us to work hard at practice?

Additionally, leagues should take note about what is happening in professional sports and be proactive with regards to providing skaters with education and protection about concussions. As much as we love the blood and beauty of our brutal sport, brain injury should be taken seriously.

"I think there's a difference between anger and aggression. With anger skaters go out haphazardly and emotional. I try to keep emotions out of it."

— Wombpunch, age 26, skating 4 years

Ego In sports

As much as sports have the potential for building character, they can also damage it. One of the downsides of sports is it can make certain athletes feel they don't just perform better than others, but that they *are* better than others. Belief in one's abilities is absolutely necessary for playing at your best but acting like you are better than others is not. Cocky, arrogant, entitled behavior will ultimately set you up to fail.

Skaters who treat their teammates as inferior or less important destroy team harmony. Treating others as if they aren't as significant as you are can be done through both words and behaviors. Something as subtle as smirking when another skater bites it or only associating with the "elite" members of your team can be seen as rude and insulting. A skater may end up alienating those she later needs to rely on.

You will always perform the worst when you have a lot to lose. If you step up to jam with your ego on the line it can set you up to choke if you make a mistake. If you've set the stage that you are the baddest of the bad then you'd better back those words up with actions. This is self-imposed pressure that is unnecessary and can be detrimental to your performance.

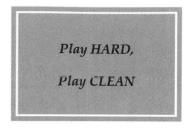

Play HARD,

Play CLEAN

It is important to separate the performer from the person. Just as a failed performance doesn't mean you are a worthless person, an awesome performance doesn't necessarily mean you are a great person. An awesome skater? Definitely. An awesome person? That depends.

- Remember to show gratitude for your abilities.

- Be thankful that you get an opportunity to play this incredible sport.

- Acknowledge the part your teammates play in your success.

- Let your awesome performance speak for you.

- Work on ways to make those around you better.

"One of the other girls on the other team got ejected. Her captain was in the box with her and they let her sit there and argue with the refs for ten minutes and then got mad because she didn't understand why she was asked to leave the building. Argued with the refs for ten minutes, told him he was a dumbass, chewed him up one side and down the other, wouldn't leave the rink, wouldn't take off her gear, sat trackside. It delayed the game, the refs were furious, it was so unnecessary."

— Punching Judy, age 47, skating 10 years

Dealing With Disappointment

One of the best ways sports can positively influence a person's character development is in allowing them the opportunity to learn how to deal with disappointment. There are many chances for being disappointed in roller derby. Here are a few examples:

- Not being selected for the allstar team

- Not passing all of your minimum skills requirements

- Losing a big game

- Getting an injury

Social skills, independence, and hope are all traits that can strengthen the ability to deal with disappointment (Weinberg and Gould, 2011). Social skills means being able to have a support group of friends, knowing how to work out conflicts with others, being flexible and having empathy.

Independence means knowing who you are and feeling like you have some control over your world. Hope means feeling like things will turn out all right in the end and that efforts will be rewarded. See Chapter 14 for more information on resilience.

Jealousy vs. Inspiration

Bonnie D. Stroir wrote a great blog about how to turn jealousy into inspiration. Jealousy comes from insecurity and lack of confidence. Inspiration is a positive feeling that will boost your confidence by making you want to excel. In her blog, Bonnie says to imagine a brand new skater watching a veteran do crossovers. She could have one of two reactions. Reaction A: She tells a friend what a show off the veteran is. Reaction B: She comments on how skilled the veteran is and asks her for help. Bonnie suggests skipping the jealous reaction and going for the inspired action.

"Praise and ask for help." "Jealousy knocks both parties down, Inspiration lifts both up."

— Bonnie D. Stroir

Mean Girls Syndrome

In her book, *Odd Girl Out*, author Rachel Simmons writes that one reason girls develop hostile cliques is to protect themselves. The girls at the top of the heap are the ones that are most afraid of being in the position of the odd girl out — the one that nobody likes. That fear motivates queen bees to surround themselves with others that are like-minded (or who pretend to be like-minded) to bolster their beliefs that they are in the right and to demonstrate a show of power.

Even though roller derby leagues have adult members, they may have some of these same juvenile problems. Those in unofficial or official leadership roles may participate in aggressive behaviors such as gossiping, bitchiness, betrayal, superiority, glaring, silent treatment, exclusivity and ganging up. Those who don't want to be singled out as not belonging to the popular group end up playing along or perhaps were on board to begin with. Skaters may feel they have to choose sides in a sink-or-swim scenario.

There are some derby veterans who may consider being mean girls just par for the course when dealing with new members. It is a sorority mentality where new pledges have to earn their respect and the privilege of belonging. So they treat newer skaters with an *I'm better than you* attitude. Why are they better? Because they thought of joining derby five years sooner? Some veterans may explain that they don't really associate with newer skaters because they might not end up sticking around so it is a waste of time. But what if the reason they don't stick around is because they were treated like lower forms of humanity when they first joined?

Some in leadership positions may end up becoming mean because they resent the hard work and responsibility that has fallen upon them. They end up taking their frustration out on others or simply may not have any genuine management skills. Most join derby to skate and knock the crap out of people and are surprised to find themselves stressed out and running a business two years later.

Some skaters may become mean girls because they feel the emotional and physical toughness required for roller derby translates to being callous and uncaring when dealing with others. Being mean is a strong behavior, whereas being kind can look and feel weak. They take what is necessary to survive on the track, and walk around in it like they are wearing a protective bitch jacket.

Regardless of why women in our sport become mean girls it detracts from everyone's game and the reputation of roller derby as a whole. If you think you may be a mean girl start the process of change by honestly answering the following questions:

Am I keeping others down/away because I am afraid of losing my position at the top?

What emotions are those around me experiencing?

Have I changed since I started derby? If so, do I like the person I've changed into?

If I lost the attitude, what am I afraid would happen?

If I was watching a movie of myself would I like the person I saw?

> *"My definition of sportswomanship is being respectful to your teammates as well as your opponents. For example, if you lay a jammer out where the jam has to be called off, it's ok to love that you timed and executed such a badass hit, but don't bask in it. It is derby and I believe there is no "I'm sorry that I hit you" but there is a level of respect by asking later if she is ok. The same goes for if you try with all your might to block someone and they don't budge then they laugh as if to say, "that's all you got?"*
>
> *— Loogie Vuitton, age 32, skating 6 years*

Ways To Improve Sportsmanship

Choosing leadership wisely. When voting on team captains and other leadership be sure to consider quality of character. Those role models will affect everyone else's behavior so pick skaters who have genuine leadership skills or are willing to learn them. It shouldn't just be a popularity contest.

There is a difference between holding a position of leadership and being a leader.

Emphasize the concept of pursuing victory with honor. The Josephson Institute Center for Sports Ethics' philosophy is that sports has its most positive impact on athletes and society when everyone plays to win. However, while trying to win is essential, "honor is more important."

161

Therefore, instead of de-emphasizing winning, teams should try to stick to ethical standards and good sporting behavior as ground rules for play. Victories attained through bad sportsmanship "are hollow and degrade the concept of sport." The most important benefits of sports come from the competition itself, not the outcome of the game.

Practice the Six Pillars of Character. Another great concept from the Josephson Institute Center for Sports Ethics is the Six Pillars of Character: Trustworthiness, Respect, Responsibility, Fairness, Caring and Citizenship. When in doubt, these can help guide your actions. Focus on who you are, rather than what you have or can do.

> *Trustworthiness.* Demonstrate integrity by being reliable and truthful.

> *Respect:* Honor roller derby and its participants with your behavior.

> *Responsibility:* Be a positive role model on and off the track.

> *Fairness:* Treat skaters fairly according to their abilities.

> *Caring:* A skater's family, job, academics and health should always be placed above needs to win.

> *Citizenship:* Establish codes of conduct for your team, coach and fans. Make sure they get followed!

Advocate for sportsmanship. During your team practices and games ask the coach to comment on personal character development and sportsmanship of skaters. During bout breakdowns make sure character and sportsmanship is one of the aspects your team's success is measured by. If your team does end of season rewards, include recognition for demonstrating aspects of sportsmanship alongside Best Blocker and Jukiest Jammer. Consider benching skaters who demonstrate terrible conduct at games, regardless of how skilled they are and how much you may need them to win.

"Pursue victory with honor." – *Josephson Institute (2014)*

Try this: Create A Code Of Conduct

Work with your team to create an individualized code of conduct. Start with general guidelines and then break them down to make them specific for your team. Remember to review it together often because it is easy to slip back into old habits. Make sure everyone understands it is their job to ensure team members stick to the code. Sometimes it seems easier to let things go to avoid conflict or to expect someone else will take care of it. But if it is a pattern of behavior it is probably not going to go away on its own and will likely get worse and spread. Not speaking up is the same thing as condoning the action. An example of what your code could look like is in Figure 12.1.

Code of Conduct

We, the _____ (team/league name), agree that it is in the best interests of all to

Always:

1.

2.

3.

Never:

4.

5.

6.

Figure 12.1 Example Team Code of Conduct

"Derby is supposed to be fun. I'm all about the winning and I'm all about the sport but you've gotta have fun. There's some girls that take it way beyond that. There's a way to hit someone and there's a way to hit someone so you're intentionally hurting them. You know what your skills level is and what others are. There are girls that hit so hard that it is ridiculous. Where their main goal is to hurt you to get you out of the game. To me that is over the top aggression."

— EMTease, age 33, skating 5 years

"The only legitimate fight I've ever been in was because another girl took me down illegally. I pretty much came up swinging. Sloppy play is one thing but when you come in purposefully to hurt me? No. It's not fun to watch, it's not fun to play. We all have jobs and we all have to pay for derby. We're not pros." *— Punching Judy, age 47, skating 10 years*

13

TEAMBUILDING

"I wish more people would approach this as a 'we' sport than a 'me' sport." — Punching Judy, age 47, skating 10 years

Most of this book is dedicated to improving the mental toughness of the individual skater. But roller derby is not an individual sport. This chapter is devoted to ways to build up the strength of the team by showing you ways to interact more successfully with each other and create the strong bonds which are necessary to raise the level of performance for you and the group as a whole.

What Is A Team?

A team is a group of people who must work together to accomplish a common goal. A team of the most talented skaters doesn't necessarily make the best team. An essential part of a good team is teamwork. That means a good team is more than the sum of its parts. Individual sacrifice and working well together are the keys to a winning team.

Weinberg and Gould (2011) identify four characteristics that differentiate a team from a mere group of people. Teams have a collective sense of identity, a sense of "we" rather than "I." Members of a team have distinctive roles and all members know what their part is. Teams also have structured lines of communication and social rules that guide members on what to do and not to do.

Team climates are dynamic, ever changing beasts. At times everyone can be getting along well and morale can be high and at other times conflict can rule the roost. Negative shifts in interpersonal relationships, having an unsuccessful season, members competing against each other for positions and individuals getting rewarded or punished can all disrupt team unity.

Ringelmann Effect

There is something called the Ringelmann Effect that demonstrates one of the things that can interfere with a team meeting its full potential. This group phenomenon was discovered by a French agricultural engineer named Maximilien Ringelmann. He measured the strength of individuals pulling on a rope and then added more people to the task. One would guess that if one person pulled 100 lbs. then two people could pull 200 lbs. and so on. But that was not the case. The more people that were added to the group, the less amount of weight each person pulled. The conclusion of this experiment is the more people there are in a group, the less effort each person will contribute. There is a loss of motivation to give 100%.

Advanced skaters can help maximize motivation for newer skaters by giving them the message that their contributions are needed. Try not to dominate the track by playing their position in addition to yours.

When individuals in a group don't put forth 100% effort because of problems with motivation, sports psychologists use the term *social loafing*. Some skaters may not give everything they've got because they feel like their teammates are handling it. This is especially true when skaters are grouped up with others of uneven skill levels. Skaters of lower levels may feel like they aren't really needed or don't have anything to contribute. When there are only two of you on the track it would become immediately apparent if one of you weren't pulling their weight. With four blockers there are more opportunities to hide in the crowd and slack off.

Another reason a skater may not give their full effort is when skating with people they don't know. A skater may choose this as an opportunity to be lazy since the group may not know their true skill level. Skating with a group you don't know can also have the opposite effect on a skater. Since you don't know the skaters you may let go of your inhibitions and take more risks. It's like how skaters may get more off the hook at afterparties when they're out of town than at home.

Ways to maximize team motivation:

- Group together with skaters of similar skill level at practice for drills and in lineups for games.

- Make sure individual contributions can be identified and evaluated. When taking turns doing drills at practice ask someone who is on the sidelines to watch your performance and give you feedback afterwards.

- Cross train in all positions at practice. Even though you may not typically jam in games, playing in this position at practice will help you to gain an appreciation for every little assist you get.

> *"Team building is absolutely vital because if you like everybody on the floor you play better, you have each other's backs more."* — Punching Judy, age 47, skating 10 years

Roles Are Important

One factor in a strong team involves roles. Roles on a team are both formal and informal. Formal roles are set by the structure of your organization. This includes referees, captains and coaches. Informal roles that may show up on a team are leader (this may or may not be the captain), enforcer, cop, social director and clown (Williams, 2006). It is important that everyone on the team know their role and accept it.

Problems can arise when roles are not clarified or are ambiguous. What is the role of fresh meat on your team? What is the role of a skater in their first game? What is the role of the captain at practice versus at games? A skater who is not the biggest, the fastest, the squirelliest or the hardest hitting may struggle with defining where they fit on the team. A coach or other formal or informal leader can help define roles for everyone. For example, a blocker who is quick but smaller in stature can have the job of "wrangler" which requires lots of speed and agility while a blocker who might not have as much speed but can deliver spleen-rattling hits can have the job of "closer" who comes in to finish the job. Have leaders assign roles for skaters who may not get as much track time as others during a game. This will help them not feel left out or confused about their contribution to the team. These skaters can help watch the penalty box, count jammer points to check for accuracy in scoring and more. Have your team give these skaters a title with a positive connotation (stay away from terms like bench warmers or 2nd string).

Problems can also come from skaters not accepting their roles or having conflict with their roles. What happens when your best jammer decides they would rather block? What happens when a skater on the team thinks they can coach better than the coach? What happens when your personal life affects the role your teammates expect you to play?

It is crucial to having a strong team that everyone has a part to play, everyone knows their part, everyone accepts their part so that they will carry it out and everyone knows what the consequence will be if they don't fulfill their responsibilities.

Team Meeting Rules

Schedule regular team meetings to discuss difficulties before they appear. Here are some suggestions for rules to follow (Weinberg & Gould, 2011):

Confidentiality. What happens at the meeting stays at the meeting.

Be constructive, not destructive. Criticize people's actions, not the people themselves.

Everyone will have a chance to speak. Make it a safe environment so that those that believe silence is safer will share as well.

Each team member must say at least one positive thing about everybody.

Don't be defensive. Be open to the opinions of others.

"I've been on a league where everybody literally fought for their positions, and the shit you would do to each other because of that? Not cool."

– Punching Judy, age 47, skating 10 years

Other Issues Teams Can Have

Cliques. Cliques are small groups of skaters who interact with one another more than other members of the team when everyone is in the same setting. These groups benefit those few involved and alienate the rest of the team. Cliques are usually formed when the team is losing, when coaches treat skaters differently or when skaters' needs are not being met. A clique is different than a group of friends because cliques are typically restrictive and focused on maintaining their status as "higher" than the rest of the team. Cliques can be extremely destructive to a team, especially when they are made up of skilled or popular skaters that others look up to. The clique can create a toxic league environment as more and more skaters emulate their negative behavior. Coaches and team members should take steps to prevent and break up cliques.

Problems with leadership. Skaters need to feel that they are being treated fairly by their captains and coaches. One issue regarding fairness is whether the way a skater views their skill level and contributions matches the way their leadership sees them. Another issue of fairness is the way leadership communicates to skaters. How something is said is just as important as what is said. Shameful and belittling comments, especially in stressful situations can be extremely damaging.

"There's people that I'm not going to be friends with outside of derby and that's ok. I can still respect them as athletes and mesh with them on the track."

– Wombpunch, age 26, skating 4 years

Team Questionnaire

Rate the following on a scale from 1 to 5 with 1 meaning you disagree with the statement and 5 meaning you agree with the statement. A higher score means a stronger team environment. There are 50 points possible. A lower score indicates there are more areas that need improvement.

1. I have a say in team decisions.

2. I can count on the coach to keep things I say confidential.

3. The coaches work well together.

4. I feel comfortable making mistakes at practice.

5. I look forward to practice.

6. My team gets along well with each other.

7. I trust my team's leadership.

8. Practices seem well organized.

9. Safety is a priority.

10. I take ownership in my team.

Try this: Establish Team Goals

One way to build a tight team is to establish team goals. Everyone on the team should be involved in setting the goals, from the freshest meat to the most seasoned vet. Your team should set short term goals that show the path to long term goals. Team goals should be specific and challenging. Make sure your team monitors its progress towards the goals. Check in on your team's progress at least monthly. When you make progress, reward yourselves!

Write down some ideas for team goals that you can present when you meet with your team. An example follows:

Make your goal specific and measurable: While everyone on my team can skate 27 laps in 5 minutes only a few can skate over 30 laps in 5 minutes. Many of us met our minimum goal and stopped pushing ourselves. Our goal is to have everyone on the team be able to skate 30 laps in 5 minutes by the end of two months.

Set short term goals that show the path to the long term goal: By two weeks from now one quarter of the team will be able to skate 30 laps in 5 minutes.

By one month from now half of the team will be able to skate 30 laps in 5 minutes.

By the end of one and a half months from now ¾ of the team will be able to skate 30 laps in 5 minutes.

By the end of two months everyone on the team will be able to skate 30 laps in 5 minutes.

How will you get there:

- We will pair up faster skaters with slower skaters at practice so they can give tips and encouragement.

- We will work on this goal at every practice.

- We will bring in a speed skating expert to give us a lesson.

- We will determine when we are strongest at practice and do our testing at that time.

- We will measure progress by quarter laps to give skaters confidence and encouragement.

Make sure your team evaluates its progress towards its goals regularly and re-evaluates those goals if needed. Remember, goals are not set in stone. Part of effective goal setting is adjusting goals if needed. Don't forget to celebrate progress, even if it is a just a small step forward!

"It is very important to me to have some sort of bonding with my teammates off the track. The teammates I see more often are ones that I skate better with without even trying. You get to know who they are as a person, not what they are made of on the track under an alias. I have never played a sport but derby so I can only say what being on a team according to derby means to me. Being part of a team in derby means having patience, an open mind and respect towards the 40 plus women you skate with. This is not a fraternity, it is not a popularity contest. You are all there for one reason, to play derby as a team. You are skating and becoming the best skater you can be for what's on the front of your jersey, not the back. It is a very selfless sport."

– Loogie Vuitton, age 32, skating 6 years

Non-Verbal Communication

Non-verbal communication gives your teammates and the other team a message. Being aware of your body language can help ensure you are saying what you want to say. Having your hands on your hips may say you have an attitude towards authority or to whoever is talking to you. It may also communicate readiness for action or aggression. Taking a knee when your coach is talking shows you are listening and what they say is important to you. There is a reason students in karate classes put their hands behind their backs when their sensei is talking — it is a non-threatening position and a sign of respect. Other non-verbal communication includes:

Sandbagging posture. This is a "bored" or "lazy" skating posture that tells everyone that you are not trying your hardest. It can be insulting to your opponents and can suck the motivation right out of your teammates.

Arm crossing. This shows people you are defensive or hiding something. It can also show that you don't care about what is going on.

Head shaking. This can give others the message that you are disagreeing or don't believe something. It can be insulting to a teammate if they see you doing this right after they made a mistake. They may see it as a sign of disgust. Head shaking communicates rejection.

Demoralized posture. This is the body language of the skater who has given up. Their head may be down or they may stop skating entirely. Make sure you show your teammates that you are still in the game so they can have motivation to fight for you and with you.

Basic Problem Solving Steps

Problem solving is about listening, understanding and finding solutions together. It is not about arguing, blaming or throwing insults. Here are the most basic concepts to keep in mind to help ensure you will be successful in solving problems with teammates:

1. Cool off

2. Tell your side of the story

3. Seek to understand the other person's side.

4. Work together to find a solution.

If conflict can't be resolved you may need to get help from coaches, captains or a mediating committee. A team meeting may be necessary where everyone lays their gripes out on the table to hash out. Sometimes the best solution is that there is no solution. Teammates may need to agree to disagree but vow to put it behind them and move forward with a fresh start. Remember, you don't have to like everyone on your team but you do need to be able to work together.

Eye-rolling. This is known to be the kiss of death for marriages so imagine what it can do to the relationships with your teammates! Eye-rolling communicates that you disagree with what a person is saying or don't like how they are saying it. It shows that you are frustrated or overwhelmed by a situation and don't even want to deal with it. It is a huge sign of disrespect.

Looking down. This is a classic sign of shame or regret. When you make a mistake during practice make sure you show through your body language that this is okay. Stand tall. And if you make a mistake during a game be extra sure not to reveal this to your opponents because you want to keep them guessing.

Lack of eye-contact. This will tend to make people feel uncomfortable because it makes them feel like you are unwilling to acknowledge them. Lack of eye-contact can also show that you are feeling embarrassed or guilty.

Frowning. Frowning signals displeasure and disapproval. Some people frown all the time and are not even aware of it. Be sure your face shows that you are happy to be at practice and are enjoying the company of those around you.

Ways To Keep Your League Drama Free

One of the biggest complaints heard from skaters about roller derby is that there is too much drama. Drama between skaters within a league that goes unresolved can result in league splits, high turnover and a general feeling of unhappiness that will affect your team's performance.

Some things that you can do to help keep this lethal negativity out of your league are:

Shut up and skate. Keep your criticism of other skaters constructive, positive and encouraging. If you can't do this then keep your mouth shut and let the coach handle the coaching.

Speak up. If you have a question or concern speak up. If you are unhappy about something you need to let your coach, captain or other leader know so it can be resolved. Most problems can be quickly and easily resolved...if somebody knows about them! Remaining unhappy without taking action will allow your anger to fester and grow inside you.

Tolerate and appreciate. You can't expect to be friends with everyone on your team. Accept this as the reality. If it turns out differently, you have received a great gift and you can be grateful. There is a difference between being friends and being able to get along well enough to work together and make your practice environment pleasant. The first is nice but the second is necessary. Look for the strengths that everyone on your team brings to the table. And remember why you are there: to skate and have fun!

Treat everyone equally.
Make sure you are not always grouping with the same skaters during drills, breaks and when gearing up and down. By spending time with everyone, including fresh meat, you will be able to form strong bonds with *all* of your teammates.

> *Negative words hold a lot more power than positive words. Once the words are out, damage may be done that can't be erased by a simple, "I'm sorry." There will have to be actions attached to the apology to show you truly mean it.*

Avoid gossip. Make your practice space a gossip free zone. Don't speak negatively about other leagues or skaters while at practice. Energy is contagious and negative vibes will spread through your league like wildfire.

Respect your leadership. Allow those in a position of leadership to lead. Imagine your league is your place of work and your leaders are your managers. How would you behave if you wanted to keep your job?

Be humble. None of us were born being badassed derby skaters and none of us will go out as badassed derby skaters. Be grateful for the skills that you may have and avoid acting egotistical. Your gifts do not make you a better person than anyone else, but your character could.

Conflict Resolution Skills

There will be times when you will have problems with other members of your league no matter how hard you try to keep things positive. Derby brings a lot of people together from different walks of life. You will meet people that you never would have if you hadn't been involved in derby. This is part of what makes it such an amazing sport. It's an opportunity for all women to find a place and succeed. But it also means there are going to be personal differences between people from time to time. Being able to resolve issues successfully will ensure that you will be able to skate without the stresses of having people on your team that you hate or that hate you. Conflicts can suck the fun right out of derby.

Resolving conflict means just that. The problem is actually "resolved." It is done. It is over. It is in the past. You have zero stress from it anymore. It is a fresh start. You are not carrying a grudge around with you. You are not pretending everything is fine when it is not. In order for a league to thrive it is crucial to be able to resolve conflicts when they arise so they don't become toxic. Here are some tips to help you to be able to resolve conflicts when and if they do occur between you and others in your league:

Talk to the person directly. Messages can change on their way to the other person. You can avoid misinformation being given on your behalf by speaking to the person you have an issue with yourself. In that same vein, don't use texting, email or social media outlets to communicate to someone you are trying to resolve a conflict with. It is important that your tone and facial expressions are part of the conversation so that the message you are giving is not misinterpreted. Besides, it takes wearing your big girl panties to talk to someone face to face.

Sleep on it. Sometimes an issue seems a lot smaller in the morning. During sleep our brains shuffle our thoughts around, problem solving and finding new ways to look at things. You may wake up and be glad that you didn't make a big deal out of something that now seems trivial or that you can now see from a different perspective.

Don't jump to conclusions. Always take the time to hear the other person's side of the story. Perceptions of a situation are highly individual. 30 people can watch the same car accident and report 30 different stories. Truly try to see things from the other person's point of view. Sometimes we are unaware of how we appear to others or how our actions are affecting others.

Listen. Nothing feels more frustrating than the feeling that we are not being heard. Screaming matches often occur because of this feeling. We think that if we raise our volume maybe the other person will understand us. We have two ears and one mouth, however, many people have a difficult time actually listening. We often are preparing what we are going to say next instead of really hearing what the other person is saying to us. A trick to help you to really listen is to ask yourself, "What is this person feeling right now?" Trying to get beyond the words to the emotions underneath can lead to real understanding.

At practice, at games, at scrimmages... dedication and commitment are contagious. What are you spreading?

Use "I Messages" to express your feelings. Saying the word "you" when confronting someone can make them feel attacked and blamed. As in "You are always doing blah blah

176

blah." Instead, use what is called an *I Message* to convey your thoughts. When we use the word "I" there is no way the other person can argue with you because you are simply stating your feelings and you have a right to them.

Improve your communication

Be honest and answer the following questions to gain insight into areas where you may need to improve your communication:

Do you try to give advice when someone is telling you their problems?

Do you stop listening once you think you understand what the other person is trying to tell you even if they aren't done speaking?

Can you recognize when you are too tired or upset to speak or listen?

Do you stop paying attention if the topic is boring?

Do you raise your voice when you want someone to pay attention to what you are saying?

Do you interrupt when you have something you want to say?

Do you find that getting in the face of the person you're talking to gets your point across?

Do you check to see if you understand what the other person is trying to tell you before you react?

Do you pretend you are paying attention when you are actually thinking about something else?

Are you listening for things you agree with or can argue against?

Are you focused more on how someone looks and sounds than the message they are telling you?

Apologize. Don't be afraid to take responsibility for your mistakes. We all make mistakes and say or do things we shouldn't. This sport is played by highly competitive, adrenalized women. We can say or do things we regret while in the heat of the moment. However, that doesn't make it okay, and it still shouldn't be acceptable. If this happens to you, take the high road and apologize. Do this as soon as possible. It can take a lot of guts to say it, but those two words "I'm sorry" can have a great impact.

Stick to one problem. Bringing up past issues or more than one issue at a time makes the problem impossible to resolve. This can happen when we have bottled things up for a long time, letting the stress build. All that past anger and frustration will look for an opportunity to come out. It may take a lot of self-control to stick to one problem, but if you want to actually resolve your conflict with someone you need to make it solvable. Don't let things build up until you are at that breaking point.

Don't make it personal. Objectifying the problem will keep it from being a personal issue and will make it easier to solve together. You can say the words, "Let's figure out how to solve this problem together," rather than, "You need to do something about your cussing." Create a physical symbol to represent the problem to further show that it is something separate from the people involved. For example, you could place a box on a table to represent "the arguing at practice." Making the problem an entity outside of any person ensures that everyone involved can look at it together from the same side.

Cool off. Be sure to calm down before you try to resolve your issue. Allow the other person time to calm down as well. When we are upset the rational parts of our brain shut down and we can't make good decisions. We need to be able to communicate clearly and respectfully and that can't happen if we are in a rage.

Let things go. If you choose not to speak up about your issue this means that you are deciding it's not a big deal and you are letting it go. Before you make a big deal about something decide if it's worth it. Sometimes it is better to suck it up a little bit to keep the peace in your league. Choose your battles. If you choose not to confront the person you have a problem with don't go complain to another teammate about your problem. By involving your teammate you have just made the problem bigger. You turned the problem from something between two people into something between three. If you are going to let things go then truly let it go. Letting things go is not the same thing as stuffing your emotions.

Time and place are important. Choosing a good time and place to talk to someone you are having a problem with can mean the difference between successful resolution and escalation. The middle of practice is not the time to get into it with someone. First of all, you don't want an audience when you are having an important talk with someone. When people are watching and listening we will tend to say or do things that may not be genuine. Having an audience increases our stress and this is a time you want to minimize stress. Second, practice should be for practicing. You don't want to disrupt other skaters' time or spread the problem to more people. Negative feelings, like positive feelings, can be contagious. If you become so upset at practice that you don't feel like you can get through it without blowing up then take a time out for yourself. Conflict resolution should be one-on-one and outside practice time if possible.

Get help if needed. Sometimes issues just can't be resolved no matter how hard you try. If you feel you have tried your best and things are not changing then it may be time to get others involved. Many leagues have conflict resolution protocols that you can follow. Coaches should also be willing and available to help out with issues since interpersonal conflicts on a team will negatively affect a team's performance.

Own your message. Be direct and honest and say "I" when it is you that has a problem, rather than "we" or "the team." Using others to reinforce your message implies weakness.

Try this: Practicing "I Messages"

Here is an opportunity to practice using I Messages to communicate. Practicing these when you are calm will help you to be able to use them when you may feel a bit heated. If you can work things out with someone one-on-one and face-to-face that is ideal. When using an I Message, first state how you feel. Nobody can argue with how you feel. Your emotions are your own. Second, tell the other person why you feel that way. They may not even know how their behavior is affecting you. Third, tell them what it is you want them to do instead. They may not do it, but at least you have given them a chance to give you what you need.

Here is an example of how to use an I Messages and a blank one for you to fill in:

I Message

I feel *unmotivated*

when you *yell at me*

because *it makes me want to give up*

I want you to *encourage me*

I Message

I feel_____

when you_____

because_____

I want you to_____

Try this: Break Down Your Games Together

Teams that learn together, grow together. It is important to always debrief your games as a team at the next practice after a game. As a group, make a list of your team's strengths and ways the team can improve for the next game. The experience should never be negative. Skaters should perceive bout break downs as an opportunity for growth. Skaters should look forward to the game breakdown and not dread it or it is not being handled right. It should feel like a key part to improving as a team.

Keep criticism constructive. Avoid blaming or put downs. Perhaps the first time you break down a game you can do it after a win so everyone is in positive spirits. Make sure to include non-skating items as well such as attitude and sportsmanship. Everyone should participate in the game breakdown. This is a great chance for newer skaters to have a lot of input into the team because they may not have had as much track time and were able to observe the game.

If your team watches game video as part of your debrief it can be a bit daunting to watch your mistakes in front of everyone. To help alleviate some of that pressure remember this: You are never as good as you think you are and you are never as bad as you think you are! Having a sense of humor and avoiding taking yourself too seriously are excellent survival skills. Looking for individual and team strengths as well as areas to improve together as a team will build bonds by keeping things honest.

Photo by DreamTeam Photography

"You can't pick your family but you can pick to play derby and gain a family!" — *Loogie Vuitton, age 32, skating 6 years*

More Ideas For Building A Badass Team!

Below are more ideas for improving the team bonds necessary for keeping derby a *want to* rather than a *have to*. Sometimes just dedicating a practice to being dorky and playing games such as Red Light, Green Light or Freeze Tag can erase a lot of tension.

Do non-derby things together as a team. Doing activities together outside of derby is great for a lot of reasons. It gives team members the opportunity to socialize, bond and have fun together. In addition, doing non-derby or non-skating activities gives team members the chance to shine that may not typically. The jukiest jammer on the team may turn out to be the suckiest bowler, be scared to jump off the rope swing or have no poker face. Some more ideas are karaoke, a yoga class, movie night, trampoline dodge ball, bake-offs or river rafting. Make sure to throw family friendly events into the mix.

Hula hoop relay. Sometimes confidence suffers when one doesn't feel they are a vital part of the team. Team building activities increase confidence because they require everyone to be involved in order to be successful. Team building activities also help a team improve communication, build trust and help skaters get to know each other better. One example of a team building activity is a hula hoop relay. This is a quick, simple activity that can be done on or off skates.

Have skaters stand in a circle and hold hands. Skaters must pass the hula hoop around the circle without breaking hands. The leader should look for Help Being Welcome (both to offer and receive), Support For Each Other, and Energy Level. Skaters must cooperate, be encouraging, have positive attitudes regarding giving and receiving help in order to be successful at this task.

Do you really know me? This is another team building activity. Have everyone on the team take turns making a statement about themselves. This statement can either be a true statement or a false statement. After a skater has made their statement the other team members can vote on whether it is true or false. Team members can keep track of their correct votes and a prize can be given at the end for the skater that knows her teammates the best. Some examples of statements are:

- I play the piano.

- I am a twin.

- I have broken my arm five times.

- I can hold my breath for two minutes.

Team playlist. Have everyone on the team pick a song to put on a team playlist and then give everyone a copy. Team members can pick songs that motivate them before games or simply songs that they love. This is a great way to learn something new about some of your teammates. Surprise! The quiet gal is a total metal head!

Team cheer. Some teams have different mottos or cheers for different situations. At the beginning of a game do a cheer that emphasizes team solidarity and gets everyone on the same page. When your team is down in points at the half you may want a cheer that increases energy, motivates and improves morale. At practice you may want a cheer to recognize ongoing effort and positive attitudes.

Have theme nights at practice. Sometimes practices become tedious when it seems like it's just week after week of serious drills. Having occasional theme nights such as animal print night, zombie night or superhero night is a great way to break up the sameness and add some lightheartedness to your practices. It's also a fun and easy way to give everyone on the team, regardless of skill level, a way to stand out.

Review your mission statement. Most teams have a mission statement. It is on their website and may be in their game programs. Bigger leagues may have it painted on the walls where they practice. Many teams, however, never actually talk about ways they can accomplish their mission. Take some time to sit down with your team periodically and break down your mission statement. Define the terms. What do the words mean to your team? Strategize together how to translate the words into specific actions. For example, say your mission statement has the word "genuine" in it. First define the word from the dictionary. Then talk about how it applies to your team. Why did it get chosen to represent you? Finally, list ways each skater can *be* genuine. Take heady, abstract or broad concepts and make them accessible as actions an individual can make on a daily basis. And if your team doesn't have a mission statement, create one!

> *"A team is a whole, it's not individuals. As in you work together, you play together, you pray together."*
>
> *– EMTease, age 33, skating 5 years*

14

PREVENT BURNOUT

Burnout is defined as "a physical, emotional, and social withdrawal from a formerly enjoyable sport activity (Weinberg and Gould, 2011, p. 496)." Can you imagine how great roller derby would be if no skaters ever quit due to burnout? The pressures involved in being a derby skater can lead to burnout. But they can often be prevented. This chapter covers the warning signs and causes of burnout and what you can do to stop it from getting in the way of a long and happy relationship with derby.

Signs and symptoms of burnout include the following:

Physical fatigue. Skaters who are well on the way to becoming burned out seem to feel tired almost all of the time. They practice feeling tired, go to bed exhausted and when they wake up in the morning they don't feel refreshed. They continuously overwork their bodies and carry around a baseline level of exhaustion that interferes with practices, games and life. Despite being in great physical shape, the burned out skater may complain about not having energy when she trains.

Frequent illnesses. Because the skater is physically run down, her immune system does not function as well as it could. The burned out skater is much more vulnerable to catching bacterial and viral infections. With a lowered resistance, the athlete may go from one cold to another over the course of a season, spending very little time feeling healthy.

Chronic injuries. The burned out skater is more vulnerable to sustaining new injuries and turning old ones into chronic injuries. This is because her body is not allowed the time to physically heal properly after an injury. As re-injury occurs, that part of her body becomes weaker and sets her up to have chronic problems.

Loss of fun. One of the defining characteristics of burnout is a total loss of enjoyment in derby. If a skater is burned out, she will stop having fun at practices and games. The initial passion and addiction she once had is fizzled out. This is visible in one's approach to practices. When you're burned out, you're no longer excited about going to train. Instead, you feel a sense of dread about having to go and once there, you can't wait for it to be over.

Loss of meaning. The burned out skater continually struggles with questions like, *What's the point?* and *Why am I doing this?* She has difficulty finding meaning in continuing to practice and play. It's as if what had initially attracted the skater to the sport has completely disappeared. The skater has lost touch with any personally meaningful goals for being involved in derby. As a consequence, apathy sets in and the individual stops caring about her efforts and results. This apathy may be experienced as boredom by the skater.

Difficulty focusing. A skater who is burned out will have trouble with focus. At practice this skater will seem all over the place. As a result, she performs at a very low level. The skater's focus may be disrupted by thoughts of wanting to be somewhere else, doing something else.

Performance problems. Skaters who are struggling with burnout may show a variety of performance problems. When working on increasing speed, a jammer may find she can't go any faster and may actually slow down. A blocker may suddenly develop an incapacitating fear and not be able to execute skills she used to be able to perform effortlessly. Something that seems like a performance problem could really be a symptom of burnout.

Behavioral problems. If a skater is having problems interacting with her teammates and/or coaches it might be a symptom of being burned out. Perhaps the skater displays a bad attitude, is overly negative or constantly instigates conflicts towards the team? These kinds of outward problems could be masking the skater's inner struggle with burnout.

Two sports psychology terms that are related to burnout are *staleness* and *overtraining*. These are both words that describe a less than desirable response to training. The desired response to training is what we hope to gain from it: to become faster, stronger and perform at higher levels. Overtraining occurs when an athlete's exercise load surpasses their ability to recover. They stop making progress and may lose previous gains made. Sometimes overtraining is done intentionally by an athlete. This process involves a period of excessive amounts of training followed by a period of rest and recovery. After the training is tapered the athlete will have adapted to the overload and be at peak performance levels. Overtraining is a different concept than *overlearning*, which is a desired state whereby an athlete knows her skills so well she does not have to consciously think about them in order to perform them.

Staleness is a negative result of overtraining: when an athlete is unable to train or perform at previously high levels. Staleness often leads to clinical depression in elite athletes.

A third term that is related to burnout is *stress*. Stress is a physiological response to situations that we perceive as threatening in some way. Recall from Chapter 6, our brain can't distinguish between real and imagined dangers and our minds and bodies will react the same way to both. If the situation does not go away it can result in stress overload.

> *"You need to find a happy medium where you can give 100%*
> *and still love derby, every practice, every bout, and every*
> *event!* – Loogie Vuitton, age 32, skating 6 years

Assessing Burnout

Researchers have developed a test to measure burnout called the Maslach Burnout Inventory (MBI). This test measures the three main characteristics of burnout.

Emotional Exhaustion. You may feel overextended and like you just don't have anything more to give.

Depersonalization. You may feel detached and like you're just going through the motions.

Low sense of personal accomplishment. You may feel like you're not competent, aren't achieving your goals or that you don't have control over situations.

The MBI contains beliefs such as *I feel like I am at the end of my rope* or *I feel very energetic*. Taking the inventory involves determining how frequently and intensely you hold the belief.

The MBI is the most widely used measure of burnout in general psychology. However, it is not geared to sports. Raedeke and Smith (2001) developed the Athlete Burnout Questionnaire (ABQ) to measure burnout in sports settings. An athlete rates each question on a scale from 1 to 5 as follows: 1= Almost never, 2= Rarely, 3= Sometimes, 4= Frequently, 5= Almost Always. The ABQ has 15 questions including:

1. The effort I spend performing would be better spent doing other things

2. I'm not into my sport like I used to be.

3. I feel less concerned about being successful in my sport than I used to.

4. I am exhausted by the mental and physical demands of my sport.

5. It seems that no matter what I do, I don't perform as well as I should.

6. I have negative feelings towards my sport.

At the end of the day a skater may simply need to ask themselves, *Am I still having fun in derby?* If the answer is *No* then figure out *Why not?* If there are things that you can change and want to change then maybe your burnout can be prevented or cured. If you aren't having fun then ask, *Why am I here?* Maybe there are enough reasons like physical fitness, identity or social life to keep you involved.

---

3 Ways People Respond to Stress

Psychologist Connie Lillas uses a driving analogy to describe the three most common ways people respond when they're overloaded by stress (Smith, Segal & Segal, 2014):

Foot on the gas. An angry, agitated, *fight* stress response. You feel heated, keyed up, overly emotional and restless.

Foot on the brake. A withdrawn or *flight* stress response. You shut down, pull away, zone out and show very little energy or emotion.

Foot on both. A tense or *freeze* stress response. You become frozen and can't do anything. You look paralyzed, but inside you are extremely troubled.

"The business side of it can drive you a little crazy and that's when its time to step back and breathe. Then you get somebody in that's new and all giddy and happy and it changes your mind a little bit."

— Punching Judy, age 47, skating 10 years

Burnout Explained

There are several theories for what causes burnout in athletes. One theory, the Commitment and Entrapment Theory, proposes athletes commit to a sport because they want to participate, because they believe they have to participate or both. Athletes who are prone to burnout feel trapped by their sport when they don't really want to stay involved but feel like they have to. This could be the skater who doesn't see any better alternative to derby, the skater whose self-identity would be lost without derby or the skater who feels pressures from teammates or family to stay involved.

Another explanation for burnout is the Cognitive-Affective Stress Model. This model says burnout occurs in four stages. In the first stage, a skater will experience the demands of a situation such as pressures to win or too many practices. In the second stage, the skater will assess the situation. In the third stage, the skater feels the physiological effects of stress such as tension, irritability and fatigue. In the fourth stage, the skater will show reactions to the physiological problems by having social or performance problems and eventually quitting the team.

More demands than resources ➡ *Stress over time* ➡ *Burnout*

To illustrate, say a skater is only allowed to play the position of blocker on her team but she really wants to be able to jam. She has asked the coach to train her to be able to jam and is told she's not "jammer material." She sees her coach putting time into bringing up the other jammers on the team and feels hurt and invalidated. She may feel this situation is unfair and awful but doesn't know what to do about it. Over time, if this situation does not change, stress will set in. The skater may become resentful of her coach or the jammers on her team. Eventually, the skater may stop playing derby all together. Each person's unique personality and motivations will determine how they appraise a given situation. Another skater might handle it completely differently. In fact, it might even be a non-issue.

Self-Determination Theory is a third model for burnout. According to this theory, if a person's basic psychological needs aren't being

189

met that could lead to burnout. People have three basic needs: *autonomy, competence* and *belonging*. Autonomy means you are able to make decisions about yourself such as a pivot deciding which play her team should run. Competence means you feel you are good at something, such as *I am a badass blocker*. Belonging means you feel socially connected to others, as in *I love being part of this team*. What are your derby needs? Are they being met?

What Causes Burnout?

Some of the factors that can lead to burnout include:

Training at a young age. Skaters who start derby at a very young age are more likely to become burned out on the sport. This likelihood will increase if they only specialize in one sport rather than trying out and playing multiple sports.

Year round training. High levels of competition mean year round, intense levels of training for most leagues. There is no time taken to physically and mentally regroup. The "more is better" philosophy may lead to burnout.

Coaching. If a coach has an autocratic, inconsistent or negative feedback style this can lead to a skater feeling burned out.

Training. Practicing or competing too much can contribute to overtraining. Repetitive drills and exercises can lead to boredom.

Time demands. Practice taking up too much time, too many travel games and not having time for family or friends could lead to burnout.

Deteriorating performances. Getting beat by people you used to beat, not being able to juke as quickly as you used to or not being able to hit as hard as you used to might make you feel burned out.

Losing. If a team has a long losing streak this can lead to burnout.

Social problems. This burnout factor could include a toxic team atmosphere or dirty play by opponents.

Financial concerns. The cost of participating in derby may cause a financial strain on your life and may lead to burnout.

Psychological concerns. Unfulfilled expectations, overemphasis on standings and feeling a lack of improvement or ability can lead to burnout.

Pressures to win. These pressures can come from coaches, family, friends or the skater herself and can lead to burnout.

Not able to meet physical demands. Skaters who can't meet the physical demands of training and competing will come under psychological and physiological stress which can lead to burnout.

Outside pressures. Having stress from things going on outside of derby like relationship problems, work or school can contribute to burnout.

Individual Differences Matter

Individual differences between skaters need to be considered when looking at who will experience burnout and who won't. Also, the reasons skaters may feel burned out will vary between individuals. For example, two skaters on the same team experience the same coach, the same teammates, the same practice schedule, the same drills, the same travel schedule and the same financial costs. However, one becomes burned out after three years in derby and another is still going strong six years later. The differences between their psychological, physical and situational characteristics will come into play when looking at who is more likely to experience burnout.

Research shows athletes with the following personality characteristics are more prone to burnout (Gould et al., 1996):

- Perfectionistic
- Self-critical
- Low self-esteem
- High need to please others

- Fear of failure
- Frustrated easily
- Competitive
- Anxious

Additionally, a skater may be experiencing several factors that could potentially lead to burnout but may only identify some of them as actually causing her to feel burned out. For example, a skater may be dealing with an injury, may not be having any fun, may not get along with some of her team, may be having problems at school, may be overtrained and have a lot of pressures on herself to succeed at derby. However, she may only see the overtraining and self-pressures as reasons for feeling so burned out she is crispy.

Preventing Burnout

Learn to cope with stress. There is a general rule for stress: either get rid of the stressor or get rid of the stress. If you want to stay involved in derby but you are finding it stressful to you, then you need to learn how to cope with the stress so it doesn't lead to burnout. This chapter has several ideas for managing stress.

Keep training exciting and fun. It's crucial that you are enjoying derby. When skaters first join derby they eat it, breathe it and sleep it. But over time that passion slowly ebbs away. Don't rely on coaches to keep practices fun. It is also your responsibility. Skaters can find ways of making repetitive drills more interesting or challenging by pushing themselves to the next level rather than simply doing what is asked. If you're not sure how to make a drill more exciting then ask your coach for ideas. Your coach should be able to make practices worthwhile to a variety of skills levels by giving instructions like, "Newer skaters can work on such-and-such and advanced skaters can try doing it backwards." Skaters should take ownership in their practices and contribute to keeping the environment fun. Simply being able to avoid taking yourself too seriously, being able to laugh at your mistakes and having a sense of humor can keep practices enjoyable. By keeping training fun and inspiring, your love of the sport will be more likely to continue.

Reframe unhelpful thinking patterns. Sometimes the way we think about a situation is what is causing it to be stressful for us. Check out Chapter 7 for more detailed information on unhelpful thinking. There is also an activity later on in this chapter that will help you to be able to recognize and reframe unhelpful beliefs.

Stay physically healthy. The mind and body do not function separately from each other. The state of one will influence the state of the other. When you know you are going to be in a mentally stressful situation be extra vigilant in how you take care of your physical health. Be sure to eat nutritious foods, get enough sleep and take it easy on drinking and smoking.

Take breaks. Trying to avoid falling behind your competition can lead individual skaters and teams to set intense, year round training schedules. It is important to take breaks from derby in the same way you take vacations from work.

Communicate. Feelings like disappointment, frustration and anxiety can become damaging to you if you keep them inside. Expressing these emotions to your teammates, coach, family and friends will help you be able to wipe your stress slate clean.

Focus on short term goals. Achieving your derby goals is part of what makes all the hard work and darker aspects of the sport worthwhile. Focusing on short term goals rather than long term goals will help you get to the rewards faster.

Develop self-awareness. Stay in tune with where you're at emotionally and be responsible for yourself. If you're having a really tough day maybe it's better to stay home that night than go to practice where things that wouldn't normally faze you become seriously irritating. This is preferable to going to practice and telling your teammates, "Stay away from me, I'm in a bad mood." Be in charge for your own emotions rather than making others take care of them for you. Recognize the signs of stress so you can be proactive and take measures to eliminate it before it becomes a bigger problem. See "How stress looks" later in the chapter.

Take recovery seriously. Playing in a game or especially in a tournament takes a physical and mental toll on a skater. If you're feeling emotionally drained following competition try getting a massage, taking a hot tub, distracting yourself by watching a movie or minimizing non-derby stressors by taking a day off from work. If you are experiencing mainly physical stressors then try eating more carbohydrates, stretching, sleeping in or participating in a low-intensity non-derby sport.

It is important to note, not all athletes who drop out of their sport are burned out and some athletes stay in their sports despite being burned out!

The Four A's

Smith et al., (2014) recommend remembering the four A's when trying to manage stress:

Avoid. Figure out which stressors in your life can be avoided and do your best to eliminate them. This can be done by learning to say "No" to people who ask you to do things. Roller derby comes with all sorts of demands on your time. When you first start out you may overcommit yourself because you are fresh with enthusiasm and want to show your dedication to your league. However, joining every committee or signing up to participate in every community service event or fundraiser will likely lead to you feeling used up fast. It might be a good idea to commit just to what is required by your league's membership contracts (i.e. you must be active on one committee and participate in one event per month) when you first join. If you feel you have time and energy for more than that you can do more! Your league would certainly appreciate it. But it does your league no good if you overdo it right away and then quit after one year because you're burned out.

Determine which things on your to-do list are "shoulds" and which are "musts." "Shoulds" are things that you feel you could be doing, or would like to do, but don't have to. "Musts" are those things that are necessary for achieving your goals in derby and life. For example, you *should* go out to have drinks for your teammate's birthday. However, you *must* do well at your job interview in the morning.

Alter. If a stressful situation can't be avoided then try to do what you can to alter it. This means being more assertive and dealing with problems. Figure out which things you can change and try to change them. If there is a drill at practice that completely freaks you out then talk to your coach about it. If someone on your team is continuously being rude to you then call them on it. Let your emotions out (respectfully) instead of bottling them up which can make your stress worse.

Adapt. If you can't avoid the stress and you can't change the stressor then try changing yourself. This means changing the way you look at things. Are you looking at the positives or dwelling on the negatives? What about derby do you really love? Find those areas and focus on them. What you feed will grow!

Accept. The ultimate change in self comes from being able to find acceptance. If you've tried unsuccessfully to avoid, alter and adapt to stressful situations and it hasn't helped then acceptance is the final answer. Accept the imperfections of others. Accept your own imperfections. Try to find the silver lining in having this situation in your life. For example, it could make you stronger or more patient. You can choose acceptance.

How Stress Looks

Some of the warning signs of stress are:

- Memory problems
- Inability to concentrate
- Poor judgment
- Seeing only the negative
- Racing thoughts
- Constant worrying
- Moodiness
- Short temper
- Agitation
- Feeling overwhelmed
- Sense of isolation

- DizzinessNausea
- Aches and pains
- Changes in appetite
- Changes in sleep patterns
- Increase in alcohol or drug use
- Nervous habits
- Constipation or diarrhea
- Grinding teeth
- Cold, sweaty palms
- Muscle tension in neck, face, shoulders

Resilience In The Face Of Adversity

Resilience is the ability to bounce back from tough situations stronger than ever rather than letting them suck the life right out of you. Why do different people respond in different ways to the same stressful circumstance? Psychologist Albert Ellis created the ABC model to help us understand our reactions to adversity. Our beliefs about the stressful situation, not the event itself, are what causes us to be upset or act in certain ways.

A is the adversity: the situation or event.

B is our belief: our explanation about why the situation happened.

C is the consequence: the feeling and behavior the belief causes.

Sometimes our beliefs about our situation aren't accurate; our beliefs may come automatically based on our individual experiences. The feelings and behaviors that result can undermine our ability to respond in a resilient way. If we can begin to uncover our beliefs, we can begin to challenge faulty or unhelpful ones. Then we can feel and act in a way that is more in line with our goals. In the book, *The Resilience Factor*, authors Karen Reivich and Andrew Shatte' developed a useful tool to help us identify some common universal beliefs associated with "negative" emotions. Negative emotions are those people typically don't like feeling such as sadness, guilt and embarrassment. By using this chart and working backwards from where we are at emotionally we can uncover our beliefs.

Common B–C Connections

Beliefs ———▶ Consequences (emotions)

Violation of our rights--Anger

Actual loss or loss of self-worth------------------------Sadness

Future threat---Anxiety, fear

Violation of another's rights-----------------------------Guilt

Loss of standing with others------------------------------Embarrassment

---

For example, let's say you are feeling embarrassed because you made a big mistake at practice. Feeling embarrassed makes you want to play in a reserved fashion so you don't mess up again. Playing conservatively at practice, however, does not help you to achieve your derby goals. You can use the Common B–C Connections chart to uncover your faulty belief. Starting with your feeling of embarrassment and working backwards you can learn that you feel that way because you believe you lost standing with your teammates. If you don't want to feel embarrassed you need to try to challenge this belief by asking yourself questions like:

- Is there another way to look at this?

- How would this look from the other person's perspective?

- What is the evidence?

Here are some ways the skater in the example could challenge her faulty beliefs:

Nobody is treating me any differently, I'm the one acting weird.

One mistake isn't going to erase years of awesomeness.

My teammates understand that everyone makes mistakes.

These reflections can help you to come up with a new belief such as, *My teammates still love me!,* which will lead to feelings of happiness. Feeling happy will lead you to give it your all at practice. Using this model can be difficult because it requires us to be emotionally honest with ourselves but it can help us learn to be resilient in the face of adversity.

Try this: Stay Centered

Centering is a practice that originated in the Japanese defensive martial art, Aikido. It is a visualization technique that teaches you to focus on the here and now. This helps you to stay stable and grounded and takes power away from stressful situations or upsetting thoughts. The more grounded and even-keeled you can remain, the less bumps in the road will phase you. Centering is not about avoiding storms, but how you weather them. With practice you can learn to ride the waves of stressful situations instead of letting them drown you. There are many centering techniques out there. The following method combines grounding with goal setting and positive affirmations.

Step 1: Find your center. Concentrate on your physical center of gravity which is about two inches below your navel. Focus your mind on this part of your body. *Feel* your center. Visualize yourself being stable and on the ground.

Step 2: Focus on your breathing. Breathe in and out deeply several times, directing your breath to your center. Fill and empty your diaphragm completely.

Skate every practice, every game, like it's your last.

Step 3: Redirect your energy. As you breathe in, picture all of your energy flowing into your center, making it strong and warm and solid. As you breathe out see your stress leaving your body. Use imagery that works for you such as picturing your energy as a glowing ball that grows bigger in your center and hurls away from you as you let it go. As you breathe in, envision your positive goals and affirmations filling you with light that radiates from your center. As you breathe out, see any negativity or barriers to your success leaving your body.

For example, breathe in *I am strong* and breathe out *Fear.* Or take in *Success* and let go of *Perfectionism.* Or fill yourself with *I am good enough* and empty yourself of *I need to please others.* With practice using this meditation you will be able to become a more centered, grounded person.

Try this: Wheel Of Life

This activity from Mindtools.com helps you to achieve balance in your life by helping you make sure you are paying enough attention to all of the important areas. The Wheel of Life worksheet (Figure 14.2) allows you to take a "helicopter view" of your life to assess it for balance. Start by coming up with the different dimensions of your life that are important to you. The worksheet provided has room for eight dimensions. If you want to draw your own wheel you can include more or fewer dimensions.

1. **Brainstorm your areas of life.** These can be roles you fulfill or other life aspects that are important to you.

2. **Write these on the spokes of the wheel.**

3. **Assess each dimension for the amount of attention it is receiving.** 0 is low and 5 is high. Different life areas need different levels of attention at different times. The concept behind this activity is to find the right *balance* of attention for each of these dimensions.

4. **Join up the marks.** Does your wheel look and feel balanced?

5. **Consider your wheel.** A balanced life does not mean getting a 5 in each life area. Inevitably, you will need to make choices and compromises because your time and energy are not unlimited.

6. **Take Action.** Are there areas that need more attention? Are there areas that are getting too much attention? Create a plan for what you need to do to regain balance.

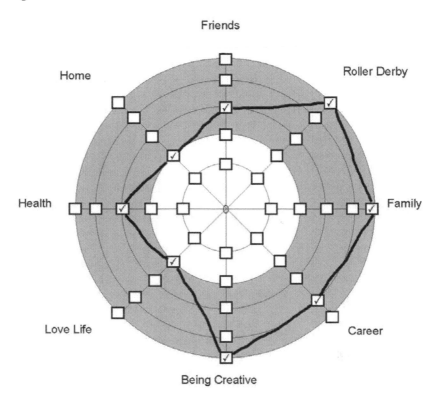

Figure 14.1 Example of a completed Wheel of Life Worksheet

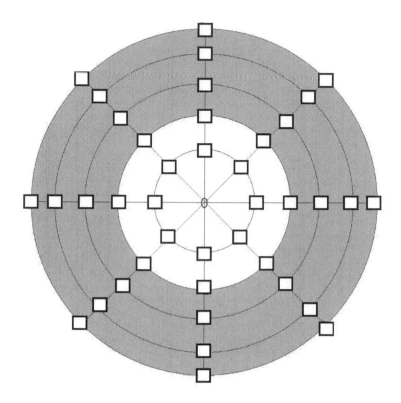

Figure 14.2 Wheel of Life. Reproduced with permission. Copyright Mind Tools Ltd. 2006–2011. www.mindtools.com/pages/article/newHTE_93.htm

Try this: Finding Solutions

One of the ways you can cope with stress is by learning how to find solutions to problems. When you can figure out what you can do about problems it can transform a ginormous mountain into a manageable molehill. Being able to take action gives us a sense of control over things. Feeling in control decreases stress.

1. First, think of a derby related problem that you have. Draw a picture of this problem in **A** (Figure 14.3). Don't worry too much about what it looks like. Stick figures are totally acceptable. Be sure to include any thoughts, feelings, dialogue or other actions.

2. Second, draw a picture of what you want things to be like in **C**. How do you want things to look when they are resolved?

3. Third, go back to the center rectangle, **B**, and draw a picture of what you can do to make this happen. Once you are done you will have a problem, a solution and a resolution. By envisioning ourselves as part of a story or movie with a beginning (A), middle (B) and an end (C) we can facilitate movement and resolution.

The emphasis here is on actions *you* can take. What can you say or do to arrive at your ideal scenario? Here are some guidelines to finding solutions:

- Is it fair to everyone involved?

- Will it work?

- Is it realistic?

- Is it something you are willing to do?

Find balance in your life!

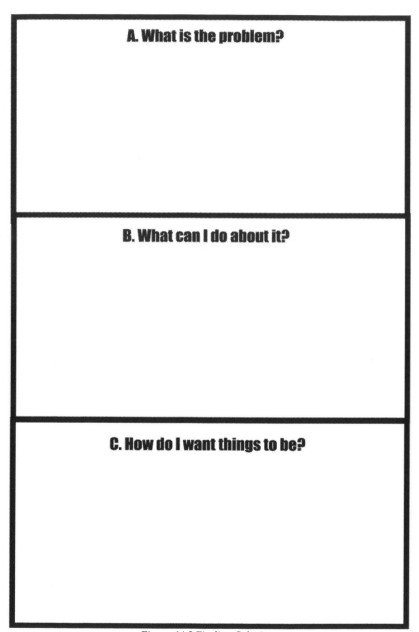

Figure 14.3 Finding Solutions

Try this: Feelings Thermometer

This activity helps you to increase self-awareness, keep things in perspective and learn to regulate your emotions. These are all skills that help you to battle stress. Figure 14.4 shows an anger thermometer worksheet, but you can create one for other emotions as well such as anxiety.

First, think of situations that make you feel calm, frustrated, angry and furious and write them on the lines next to the thermometer. A situation that would make you the angriest you've ever felt in your life should go at the top. These can be hypothetical situations or things you've actually experienced. A situation that wouldn't make you feel angry at all would go at the bottom. The intensity levels for anger are shown on the thermometer with 1 (no anger) being at the bottom and 10 (the most anger you could possibly feel) at the top. You can come up with your own words to describe the different levels of anger if these don't fit for you.

Second, take some time to think about how these different levels of anger feel in your body and mind. How does it feel to be at a level 7 compared to a level 3? People typically experience more mental and physical tension the more upset they feel.

The next time you find yourself in a situation where you are getting angry you can check in with yourself to see if you are reacting appropriately or overreacting. You can do this by first deciding where on the scale the situation should fall. Is it so serious that it is an 8? Is it a 4? Or is it only a 2

Then you can see if the intensity level of your reaction matches the situation. You should meet a 6 situation with a level 6 in emotional intensity. Do you react with an 8 to any situation regardless of how serious it is? If you find yourself overreacting you can work to calm by using strategies such as helpful self-talk, walking away, breathing or distracting yourself.

1. What makes you feel calm, frustrated, angry or furious? The most anger you could possibly feel is a 10, the least amount of anger is a 1.

2. The next time you find yourself feeling angry, determine where on the scale from 1 to 10 the situation falls?

3. If you find you are overreacting or underreacting, adjust your emotional intensity up or down to match the situation.

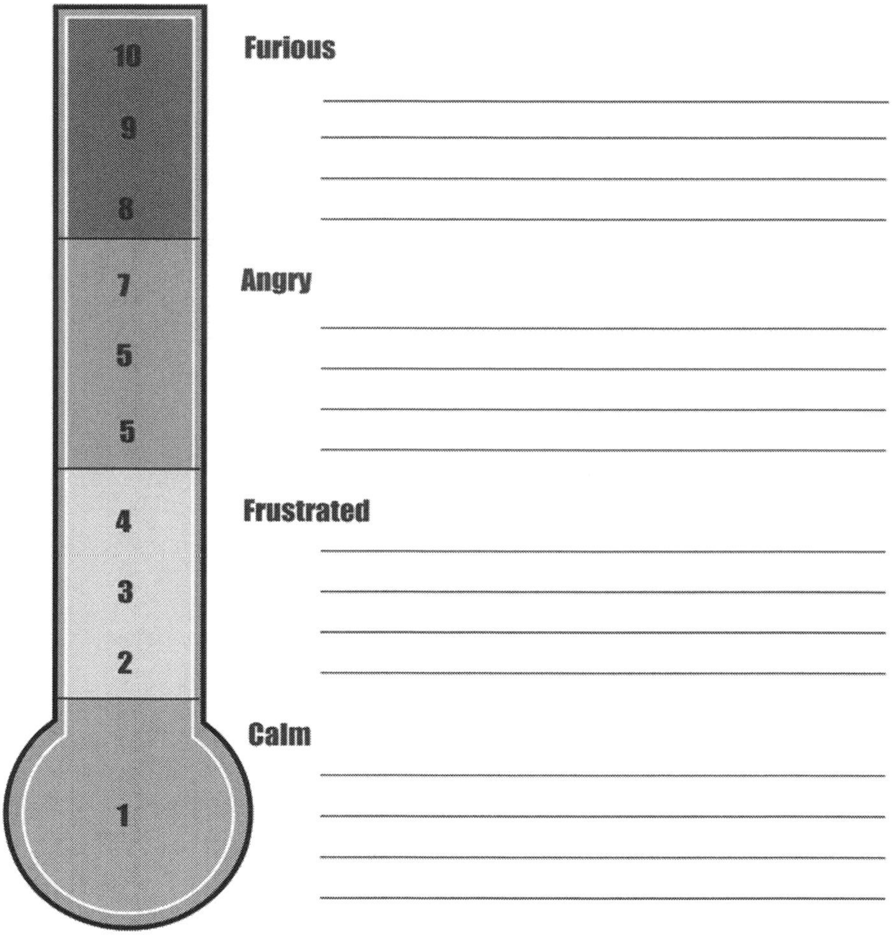

Furious

10
9
8

Angry

7
6
5

Frustrated

4
3
2

Calm

1

Figure 14.4 Anger Thermometer

"When the attitude and the environment is so negative. I had to step back and take a break and let things simmer down."

— EMTease, age 33, skating 5 years

15

LIFE AFTER DERBY

The topic of retirement from derby can be an emotionally charged one. When asked if they think about retiring, most skaters say "hell no." However, at some point even the most dedicated skater's competitive roller derby career comes to an end. Reasons for retiring vary from skater to skater. Skaters also experience this transition in various ways. For some it isn't a big deal at all. However, for others it can be a very upsetting and negative time. This chapter is dedicated to helping skaters make the transition out of competitive playing as smooth as possible when and if the time comes.

"Oh crap, I'm already in my 30's. I hope I can last for a while." — Pinktastic, age 31, fresh meat

There Are Lots Of Reasons For Retiring

Sometimes retirement comes unexpectedly from an unforeseen negative life event. A skater may be forced to retire because of a job loss, serious injury or other issue. Not only will the skater have to deal with the life issue, they may also be struggling with the loss of derby. Sudden, unforeseen, unwanted retirement can be devastating.

Unexpected retirement can also come from a positive life event such as pregnancy. Many skaters decide to return to derby after having a baby but some decide to focus on their families. Even though the change is good and wanted, the skater may experience some level of grieving because they are giving up derby. Mixed emotions are completely normal.

Retirement may also be a planned event. A career change, moving or going back to school may mean needing to stop playing derby. A skater may also decide they want to retire to focus on other hobbies or interests. The truth is, derby takes up a lot of time. A skater may retire because she feels her body has had enough abuse. The physical demands that derby places on the body are incredible. With planned retirement it is possible to know which season or game will be your last.

The primary reason athletes retire is age, or more specifically, the decline in performance due to advancing age. While the answer to the question, "How old is too old to play roller derby?" is usually dependent on individual factors, it is likely that at some point you will feel that it is time to stop competing at least at a highly intense level. Our bodies become more prone to injury, it takes longer to heal and self-preservation may start to seem like a good idea. With that in mind, there are skaters out there playing into their 50's and beyond!

Reasons for retirement:

- Work
- School
- Lost motivation
- Politics of derby
- Decrease in performance

- Finances
- Age
- Injury
- Not being picked
- Family

Mourning The Loss Of Derby

Retiring from derby can be experienced as a loss for many skaters. Depending on how big a part of the skater's life derby was, the loss can be anywhere from insignificant to life shattering. How strongly a person identifies as a derby girl will determine how big a loss she experiences retirement to be. For the skaters that see derby as a fun hobby that is a small part of their lives, the transition out of competing will be smooth. For the skater that lives, breathes, sweats and bleeds derby, the transition may be much more painful.

Elizabeth Kubler-Ross suggested that people who go through a loss experience five stages of grief. Not everyone experiences all five of the stages and the stages do not have to occur in any particular order. But some of the things you might feel are:

Denial. This stage includes feelings of shock, numbness, and disbelief. When loss first comes, most of us have a hard time believing that it is really happening. It's not that we're denying that the loss of competitive derby has *actually* occurred, but rather, it's a sense of, *I just can't believe I'm not going to be skating anymore.* Yet, the feelings of this stage also protect us. If we were to take in all the emotion related to the loss right away, it would be too overwhelming. Instead, our body and mind have a little time to adjust to the way things are now without derby. Part of the denial stage is also to tell our story over and over. This is one of the best ways to deal with bad things and also a way for us to make it real. Eventually, we may begin asking questions such as, "How did this happen," or "Why?" This is a sign that we are moving out of the denial phase and into the feeling and healing process.

Anger. Anger can present itself in a variety of ways. You may feel angry at your teammates, at your family, at roller derby, at the world or at your body for betraying you. Anger can be a difficult emotion to cope with. Some will express anger easily and toward anyone or anything, but many of us will suppress the anger, keeping it bottled up or even turning it inward toward ourselves. Anger is a natural response to loss. If we're able to identify and label our anger, it can help us express it in healthier ways that don't hurt others or ourselves. Saying, "I'm angry," and letting yourself feel that anger is part of the healing process.

But derby is what makes me cool!

Bargaining. With bargaining, there's a sense that we just want life back to the way it used to be. We wish we could go back in time, before the injury, perhaps see something we didn't see. We may also feel guilty, focusing on thoughts of *If only…* Bargaining can begin before the loss occurs or after. If retirement was anticipated, such as in the case of hanging up the skates due to feeling like you're getting too old, bargaining may have been going on for a while. *I wish I would have started skating five years earlier!"* If retirement was sudden, we may wish we could go back in time and change things. Bargaining keeps us focused on the past so we don't have to feel the emotions of the present.

Sadness. Eventually, grief will enter on a deeper level, bringing with it feelings of emptiness and sadness. We may feel like we don't care about much of anything. Others around us may try to help get us out of this depression. We have to let ourselves feel the pain, loss, grief and sadness even if that seems hard. As Kubler-Ross encourages, "Make a place for your guest. Invite your depression to pull up a chair with you in front of the fire, and sit with it, without looking for a way to escape. Allow the sadness and emptiness to cleanse you and help you explore your loss in its entirety." This part of the grief process can last for some time. There's no set time limit for the emotions of grief. Be patient with yourself and remember that feeling the sadness is the way out of it.

Acceptance. The experience of sadness is what leads to acceptance. Many people mistakenly believe that acceptance means we are cured or okay with the loss. But this isn't the case at all. The loss may forever be a part of us though we will feel it more some days than others. Acceptance simply means we are ready to try and move on. We are ready to live *fully* in a life without playing roller derby.

Understanding the 5 Stages of Grief can help us realize our grief is normal and help us navigate the varying thoughts and feelings we each experience. Mostly, understanding the 5 Stages of Grief can reassure us that we are not alone in our experience. Grief is one experience we all have, or will have, in common. That means we have plenty of experienced souls to whom we can turn for support and guidance getting through retirement.

> *"When the time comes you'll know. Your body is trying to tell you enough is enough."*
>
> *— EMTease, age 33, skating 5 years*

Plan For Retirement Before You Decide To Retire

In order to have an easier transition to life after derby be sure to plan for retirement well before you think you will retire. Doing this will also help you have a safety net in case you have to retire unexpectedly.

What role will derby play in your life after you retire? Decide how much involvement in derby you want to have after retirement. Some skaters completely separate themselves from the sport, focusing entirely on other areas of their life. Some skaters continue to be involved as fans. Some skaters consider the derby bonds they formed to be bonds for life and remain close friends with former teammates. Some skaters stay very active in derby: volunteering, announcing, fundraising, coaching or finding other ways of being involved.

Respect other parts of your life during your competitive years. Make sure you have meaningful possibilities to consider when you retire by keeping your life balanced while you are still involved in derby. Be sure to spend enough time with friends, hang out with your family or focus on your career.

Get your supports ready. Have the support of at least one close person immediately after you retire. This could be a parent, coach, close friend, teammate or other loved one. If there are specific ways they can help you, let them know.

Figure out what's next. Focus on new areas of interest while still competing in derby so that you can jump right into new activities following retirement. Take some classes, try some new sports or check out some other hobbies. Think of the transition out of competition as a positive opportunity to grow and develop in new ways. Find new ways to get your thrills, maybe without the spills.

Keep exercising. Your body is used to a high level of physical activity. You worked hard to get in this shape so be sure to stay active and keep exercising! It will be good for your mind and your body to maintain the gains you've made. You don't want to be hating yourself because you let that fantastic derby butt get saggy.

Share your experience with others. Get together with others who are also going through the retirement transition. Hear about their experiences adapting to a different lifestyle. Too many skaters quit derby and disappear. Think about starting an alumni club!

> *"Until I actually break I don't think I'll quit. I think I will play until literally I can't play anymore."*
>
> *– Punching Judy, age 47, skating 10 years*

> *"I used to think derby was my only source of happiness until I recently had a high ankle sprain. Since I couldn't skate it out anytime soon, or skate through the pain, I was forced to find other things to do. Like what "normal" people do. Go to concerts, hang out with non – derby people. Gasp! There is such a thing! So retirement is not such a bad thought for me anymore. I will hang up my skates one day but today is not the day! I will play until I feel like I can no longer be my best because I know there will be life after derby. I will have the best stories to tell my grandkids and roommates at the nursing homes." – Loogie Vuitton, age 32, skating 6 years*

16

MORE MENTAL TOUGHNESS STUFF

The chapter contains information on miscellaneous mental toughness topics from eating disorders to self-hypnosis.

EATING DISORDERS

Roller derby, more than a lot of sports out there, has a place for women of a variety of different shapes and sizes. The acceptance and need for skaters who are skinny, big and everything in between is part of what makes roller derby an empowering and powerful sport. However, the pressures of sports combined with an existing cultural emphasis on thinness increases the chances that an athlete, regardless of the sport they participate in, is at higher risk of developing disordered eating than the general population (Matsumoto, 2014). Additionally, female athletes suffer from eating disorders at a much higher rate than male athletes. This purpose of this section is to provide education about eating disorders as a way to help prevent them for you and your teammates.

Problems with eating can be seen as occurring on a spectrum with body image issues at one end, disordered eating in the middle and full blown eating disorders at the other end. Body image problems and disordered eating are risk factors for developing eating disorders. One type of eating disorder is Anorexia nervosa. The characteristics of the life-threatening disorder, Anorexia nervosa include:

- Deliberate self-starvation

- Refusal to maintain body weight at or above 85% of what would be normal for age and height

- Intense fear of gaining weight or becoming fat even though underweight

- A distorted view of the way one's body weight/shape is experienced

- Amenorrhea (absence of at least 3 periods in a row)

Bulimia nervosa is also a serious life-threatening disorder and includes the following characteristics:

- Recurrent episodes of binge eating

- The binges are followed by purging (usually self-induced vomiting but can be laxatives, excessive exercise, diuretics or fasting)

Binge Eating Disorder is another type of eating disorder that is characterized by recurrent binge eating without the purging aspect. Disordered eating is having habits such as excessive avoidance of certain types of food, eating fewer calories than needed for sports activity and occasional binging and purging. Disordered eating activities impair an athlete's ability to function optimally but don't meet the criteria for an eating disorder diagnosis. A few unofficial terms used in the sports community are *drunkorexia*: self-imposed starvation or bingeing and purging combined with alcohol abuse; *orthorexia* nervosa: taking concerns about eating healthy foods to dangerous or obsessive extremes; and *anorexia athletica*: when athletes have eating disorder symptoms that are not severe enough to warrant the full diagnosis (Matsumoto, 2014).

Here are some signs and symptoms of eating disorders:

- Perfectionism

- Difficulty handling days off from exercise

- Avoiding water or drinking water excessively

- Preoccupation with food

- Light-headedness or dizziness

- Overuse injuries

- Frequent weighing

- Anxiety

- Negative comments about weight or being fat

- Training even when sick or injured

- Abdominal pain

- Hoarding food

- Disappearing after meals

- Excessive eating without gaining weight

- Numbness and tingling in limbs (due to electrolyte imbalance)

- Slowed heart rate and low blood pressure

- Longer recovery time needed in between practices and games

- Decreased concentration, energy, muscle function, coordination and speed

- More frequent strains, sprains or fractures

- Decreased body temperature and being sensitive to cold

- Increased isolation, impatience and crankiness

- Prolonged training above and beyond what is required for the sport

- Ritualistic eating

There are personal factors that put an athlete at risk for developing an eating disorder.

Being involved in endurance sports or sports where appearances are important. Skaters playing the jammer position may feel an intense amount of pressure not only due to the physical and strategic demands of the position but because of the attention from the audience. Skaters may feel this pressure when they are playing other positions as well, but the jammer position has more potential due to the "performer" aspect.

Not balancing output and input of energy. If a skater is burning high levels of energy they need to replace it with equally high levels of energy (calories) or they are going to lose weight.

Performance anxiety, fear of failure. Having an appropriately lean physique can help an athlete to maximize speed. A newer skater, seeing a faster and thinner jammer on the track may mistakenly put too much emphasis on losing weight in order to reach their performance goals. They may determine the jammer is faster because she is thinner without considering other factors such as her training. This thinking can put them at risk for an eating disorder because if they lose weight and still aren't performing where they want to be they may think it is because they didn't lose enough weight. A thin athlete is not necessarily a strong athlete because too much weight loss can take away power and strength.

History of trauma, sexual abuse, genetic history of addiction, chronic dieting. Individuals with a history of these problems may not have had the opportunity to develop healthy coping strategies.

Athletes are prone to eating disorders because excelling relies on the state of their bodies. The drive for a perfect performance can become tied into having the perfect body. Distorted thoughts then develop about food, weight and body image. These beliefs in turn lead to extreme practices in dieting and workouts. One way to prevent eating disorders is to keep exercise at a healthy and appropriate level. Sports should be seen as a lifetime pursuit which means taking good care of your body so you can be active for a long time. Be flexible in scheduling workouts and if you have to miss one because life gets in the way it is okay. It doesn't need to be made up. You can just get back on your regular workout schedule as soon as you can. Several factors are part of a great athletic performance: genetic gifts, muscle mass, confidence and motivation. These factors have more power with great nutrition and proper hydration. The following are more ways to prevent eating disorders for you and your teammates:

The American College of Sports Medicine came up with the term, the Female Athlete Triad, to describe the three interrelated symptoms of disordered eating, menstrual irregularity and low bone mass seen in athletic women.

1. Discourage dieting because it is the primary precursor to disordered eating.

2. Have a dietician speak to your team about how to eat in ways that maximize performance. A crucial aspect of proper sports nutrition is replenishing the muscle and liver's glycogen stores. 15 to 60 minutes after practice or games a skater should eat a snack or meal that contains carbohydrates and protein. This will repair the body and provide energy for the next workout.

Some ideas for an after game/practice snack are:

1–2 cups chocolate milk

Yogurt with fruit

Energy bar that contains nuts

Peanut butter and jelly sandwich

Hydration is essential to maintain normal physiological functioning and cool the body. Some signs of dehydration include muscle cramps, nausea, weakness, dizziness and fatigue. Hydration for a game should start that morning.

3. Banish negative comments about size/shape from your practice environment. Be careful of subtle messages about the idealization of certain body types such as, "She has the perfect body for this sport."

4. Be aware of possible mental discomfort that some on your team might have about uniforms. Form fitting or revealing uniforms may increase body consciousness, body dissatisfaction and body comparison with others.

5. Focus more on fitness and less on body weight by looking for ways to enhance performance through endurance or strength training.

6. Weight is what it is and it is up to the coach to position athletes appropriately instead of having them try to manipulate their weight.

7. If there are concerns that a player does not meet the health requirements to be able to join safely in practice, have them get clearance from their medical doctor prior to participating. This keeps the emphasis on health

and all that it encompasses, inside and outside of a person, rather than just on appearances.

8. Know that eating patterns can be contagious in groups of women. Take care of your teammates by being a healthy role model and insist your teammates do the same for you.

9. Having a coach who focuses on factors that contribute to success such as motivation and enthusiasm, rather than body weight or shape, can help protect an athlete from developing an eating disorder. Coaches who have a positive approach and focus on the person over the performance also help. Additionally, having teammates with healthy attitudes about size and shape can be a protective factor.

10. Find the balance between weight and performance. Strive for a point where you are feeling your strongest and able to execute derby skills to the maximum of your ability. This is highly individualized because everyone's muscle composition is different.

Myths And Misconceptions About Eating Disorders:

Purging will help you lose weight. Half of what is eaten usually stays in the body after self-induced vomiting. The weight loss from laxatives is temporary. This why many people with bulimia are average or above average weight.

People with anorexia never eat. If someone didn't eat at all they would die in a matter of weeks. People with anorexia eat really small portions, extremely low-calorie foods or strange food combinations. Some may eat candy bars in the morning and nothing the rest of the day. Others may only eat lettuce and mustard every two hours.

Anorexia is extreme dieting. Anorexia has nothing to do with dieting though a history of chronic dieting can be a risk factor to developing anorexia. Anorexia is a life-threatening medical/psychiatric disorder.

Eating disorders are all about appearance and beauty. Eating disorders are related to emotional issues such as control and low self-esteem. Though concerns about appearance can be a precursor for an eating disorder the behaviors would not be continued past the person's initial "target" weight if they were not maintained by other factors.

Males with eating disorders tend to be gay. Sexual orientation has no relationship to developing an eating disorder. Many men who develop eating disorders are athletes with performance pressures connected with "making weight" for sports such as boxing, wrestling or weight lifting.

A person cannot die from bulimia. A person with bulimia can be at risk for sudden death because of the impact on the heart and electrolytes from excessive exercise and laxative abuse.

Do You Have Disordered Eating?

The following questions come from the book, *Women Afraid to Eat*. If you answer yes to more than three you may have disordered eating (Berg, 1999).

1. Do you regularly restrict your food intake?

2. Do you skip meals regularly?

3. Do you often go on diets?

4. Do you count calories or fat grams, weigh or measure your food?

5. Are you "afraid" of certain foods?

6. Do you turn to food to reduce stress or anxiety?

7. Do you deny being hungry or claim to feel full after eating very little?

8. Do you avoid eating with others?

9. Do you feel worse (anxious, guilty etc.) after eating?

10. Do you think about food, eating and weight more than you'd like?

Eating disorders can cause dehydration, electrolyte imbalance, constipation, reduced muscle mass, osteoporosis, peptic ulcers, erosion of tooth enamel, type II diabetes, brittle hair and nails, dry skin, gall bladder disease, high cholesterol, malnutrition and other physiological problems. Eating disorders are life-threatening. Cardiac arrest and suicide are the leading causes of death in people with eating disorders.

If you or one of your teammates is at risk for developing an eating disorder or currently has an eating disorder they need to talk to a medical doctor. Coaches should be involved in approaching a team member who may be suspected of having an eating disorder and recommend they seek help. It is important to avoid giving the skater the feeling that they are being attacked or shamed. Make sure the meeting is focused on behaviors and performance rather than on eating habits or weight. The eating disorder should be treated like an injury rather than an emotional issue. Coaches should let the athlete know they need to be healthy to be able to skate.

PSYCHING OUT AN OPPONENT

Psyching out an opponent is probably what comes to mind for a lot of people when they think of sports psychology. However this is just a small portion of the mental game. When you successfully psych out your opponent you are able to psychologically get them into a position where you can dominate them physically. Some might call these techniques dirty tricks. Rather than place judgment on the practice of trying to psych out your opponent, some different methods will be presented and the reader can decide for herself which, if any, she would want to try.

Have a secret stash of weapons. This one is a game strategy. Don't use your top jammers right away in a game. Your opponents will establish a tempo in reaction for what your team is bringing. Wait long enough for them to get comfortable and then unleash your beasts. Having to adjust their game strategy unexpectedly may cause some chaos on their bench that you can exploit.

Make your opponent angry. There are lots of ways to do this but in an attempt to maintain consistency with the chapter on sportsmanship we will try to stick with methods that aren't too dickish. You can try to be the ref of your opponents by constantly telling them real or imaginary penalties they are committing. It isn't illegal and if you keep the language clean it doesn't fall into the category of bad sporting behavior. After a while, your opponent may become so angry and frustrated it will cause them to lose that razor edge of focus they need to play their best. This technique sometimes has the added advantage of actually getting them sent to the box on some of these imaginary penalties because a less seasoned referee may hear you make the call and then call it themselves.

Screw with the start of game time. This is a method of psyching out a whole team. By delaying or rushing the start of the game you disrupt your opponents' energy management process by preventing them from getting their energy to peak at the right moment. If you rush the start they may not be ready to peak. If you delay the start they may peak early and not be able to get energized again.

Be a mystery. Don't reveal your talents to your opponents during warm up time. Teams often use this time to scope out the threats they will be facing on the opposite team. Don't stand out. Don't let them know what your talents are. Or if you're super-duper skilled, do the opposite and intimidate the hell out of your opponents by pulling off some amazing stuff during warm up. Just be sure you can back it up come game time.

Put the pink elephant in their head. What's the first thing you think of when you're told not to think about a pink elephant? Did you just think of a pink elephant? Suggestion is very powerful. As has been covered elsewhere in this book, thinking about something makes it more likely that it will happen. That is why it is so crucial to always think of the way you want things to play out, not the opposite. Use this concept to your advantage by suggesting to your opponent the things you want them to do. Some ideas are:

- *You don't pull your hits at all anymore, nice work!* It seems as if you just gave a compliment but it is actually a counter-compliment. The idea that you've planted is **pull your hits**.

- *The last team we played were back blocking like crazy, thanks for not doing that.* This puts **back blocking** into your opponent's head.

- *You're doing a really great job of not cutting the track!* Now your opponent will think about **cutting the track**.

Play it cool. Someone who is anxious will move around a lot because their nervous system is primed and charged. If your opponent is already uncomfortable it will be easier to psych them out. Keep verbal contact to a minimum to imply aggression. If you have to talk to her do so only in monosyllabic grunts. Stand up tall and give her a silent stare. Make your opponent think you have zero cares to give.

Mess with their momentum. Psychological momentum is when a team feels a surge in confidence, morale and energy that allows them to play to the best of their abilities. There are lots of opportunities during a game for a team to gain psychological momentum: getting a power jam, getting an official review in their favor, getting pumped up by fans, pulling off a really cool play and more. The team on the other side of things may experience a downturn in their own psychological momentum at the same time and is not able to play to their full potential. When a team has the momentum of the game going for them and capitalizes on it, the game may be theirs for the taking. The opposing team can try to prevent this by breaking up their momentum. One way to do this is to call a team time out or ask for an official review. Nothing kills the momentum of a game like a lengthy zebra huddle. A dishonest way of taking away the other team's momentum is by faking an injury that gets the jam stopped when the other team is annihilating you and you don't have lead jammer.

Photo by Robert Massey

Trash talking is another way to psych out your opponent. It is defined as, "insulting or boastful speech intended to demoralize, intimidate, or humiliate someone, especially an opponent in an athletic contest" (Oxford, 2014). Trash talkers attempt to psych out their opponents by filling them with fear and frustration. The fear can paralyze an opponent's game and the frustration can cause an opponent to make mistakes or even retaliate physically, getting them thrown out of games. Some trash talkers do it to motivate themselves or just for shits and giggles. Trash talk usually involves belittling the skill or toughness of an opponent or praising one's own ability. Trash talk can affect the outcome of competitions, can lead to violence and is not always in good fun.

Here is a rundown of some of the most famous trash-talkers in professional sports history:

Richard Sherman, Seattle Seahawks. Richard Sherman describes his talk and attitude as "swagger." In 2013 he told Vikings receiver Cordarrelle Patterson, "You not strong enough, you need to lift a little more."

Muhammad Ali, professional boxer. Muhammad Ali would often win fights before even stepping into the ring with his poetic words. His words not only pumped him up but rattled his opponents. Fans and press loved to hear him trash-talk and it is likely this attention further boosted his confidence. "Float like a butterfly, sting like a bee... his hands can't hit what his eyes can't see." Once he told George Foreman in the middle of a fight, "Is that all you've got?"

Terrell Owens, 49ers, Eagles, and Cowboys. He was the pre-eminent touchdown celebrator, putting it in the other team's face with flamboyant style every time he scored. This tactic disrespected his opponents and may have gotten in their heads, causing them to over-target Owens and not pay as much attention to the big game picture.

Larry Bird, Celtics. Telling an opponent your plans can actually end up working for you if it gets into their heads. Larry Bird once told his defender, Xavier McDonald, "Xavier, I'm gonna get the ball right here. I'm gonna take two steps back and hit a fade away jumper in your face." And that is exactly what he did. The best way to deal with trash talkers is to avoid getting engaged with them. Just stay focused and do your thing.

Reggie Miller, Pacers. Reggie Miller was a master at being able to get his opponents to lose their cool and make irrational decisions based on emotion. In the 1993 playoffs he targeted John Starks. "I made it a mission, I'm gonna embarrass this kid." Miller's use of non-verbal trash talk (continually throwing elbows) caused Starks to get so irritated that he head butted Miller. Miller took a dive and Stark was ejected from the game.

Mike Tyson, professional boxer. Mike Tyson tried to strike fear in the minds of his opponents with his crazy, bloodthirsty trash talk. "There's no one that can match me. My style is impetuous, my defense is impregnable and I'm just as ferocious. I want your heart! I want to eat his children!"

Serena Williams, professional tennis player. "We all know who the real No. 1 is. Quite frankly, I'm the best in the world." Serena Williams claimed this after being unseated by Dinara Safina in 2009. Examples of trash talking by professional women in sports are difficult to find. Research has shown that it occurs in men's sports much more frequently than in women's sports but that the more aggressive the sport, the more trash talk that occurs (Rainey, 2008).

Bobby Riggs, 1940's professional tennis player. In one-on-one battles trash talking can get under an opponent's skin or get in their heads which can take them out of the game. However, trash talking can also mean an athlete is wasting time and energy that they need to be putting into their performance. This happened to Bobby Riggs. In 1973, the self-proclaimed "male chauvinist pig" tennis player said he could beat any top women's player because women's tennis was inferior to men's. Billie Jean King accepted his challenge and kicked his ass.

It should be noted that all of these techniques put the focus on your opponent and not on you playing your best. Nothing will psych you out more than playing against an opponent that no matter what you do or say is totally unaffected by you. So the best psych out method of all may be to put all these games aside and be that skater.

SUBSTANCE USE

Despite the possibility of many negative consequences including decreased performance and serious health risks, many athletes use substances. These are the reasons they do so (Weinberg & Gould, 2011):

Physical reasons. Athletes may use substances to look better, perform better and feel better when injured.

Social reasons. Athletes may drink, smoke, or take performance-enhancing or other drugs to be accepted by peers, seek thrills and out of curiosity.

Psychological reasons. Athletes may use substances, typically recreational ones, to deal with stress or escape from pressures and to gain increased self-confidence.

Substances fall into two categories: performance-enhancing drugs and recreational drugs. Performance-enhancing drugs are any substance an athlete takes to improve their performance. This includes anabolic steroids, human growth hormone (hGH), stimulants and diuretics. Anabolic steroids are taken to increase muscle mass and strength and improve the body's cosmetic appearance. When using anabolic steroids, an athlete can train harder with shorter recovery times. Some athletes who take anabolic steroids also like the feeling of aggression it gives them. The main anabolic steroid hormone produced by your body is testosterone. Side effects include male traits in females such as facial hair or a deeper voice, severe acne, heart problems, depression and "'roid rage." Research has shown a significant increase in anabolic steroid use in young females (Yesalis & Bahrke, 2014).

Recreational drugs include alcohol, marijuana, caffeine, opioids, stimulants, sedatives and hallucinogens. The Diagnostic and Statistical Manual (DSM-5), describes substance use as occurring on a spectrum from not a diagnosable problem, to mild, moderate and severe. As an example, here are the symptoms for an Alcohol Use Disorder:

Mild: The presence of 2 to 3 symptoms

Moderate: The presence of 4 to 5 symptoms

Severe: The presence of 6 or more symptoms

Performance-enhancing drugs, effects and risks

Type	Definition	Use	Risks
Peptide Hormones including hGH	A hormone that has an anabolic effect	Improved muscle mass.	Joint pain, muscle weakness, fluid retention, carpal tunnel syndrome, diabetes, and high blood pressure.
Erythropoietin	A type of hormone used to treat anemia in people with kidney disease.	Increased production of red blood cells and hemoglobin causes improved movement of oxygen to the muscles and improved endurance.	Stroke, heart attack and pulmonary edema
Diuretics	Drugs that change the body's natural balance of electrolytes.	Water loss can lower an athlete's weight and help them to pass drug tests by diluting their urine.	Dehydration, muscle cramps, potassium deficiency, fainting, drop in blood pressure, heatstroke, and death.
Creatine	Supplement available over-the-counter.	Helps muscles create more adenosine triphosphate (ATP) which stores and transports energy in cells. It helps for quick bursts of activity like sprinting.	Stomach cramps, weight gain, diarrhea, nausea, dehydration, damage to kidneys and liver at high doses.
Stimulants	Caffeine, ephedrine, pseudoephedrine, and amphetamines are common stimulants.	Gives increased energy, aggression, and alertness.	Addiction and tolerance, heatstroke, dehydration, psychological problems, nervousness and irritability, heart palpitations, tremors, stroke, convulsions, weight loss, heart attack, and death.
Beta-blockers	Drugs that lower blood pressure and decrease heart rate.	Steadies nerves.	Slowed heart rate, depression, nausea, vomiting, weakness, tingling, numbness, light-headedness, and bronchial spasm.
Narcotic Analgesics	Drugs that kill pain.	Reduced pain.	Constipation, drowsiness, fear and anxiety, dry mouth, difficulty concentrating, physical and psychological dependence, and the "itchy bitchy" syndrome.
Anabolic Steroids and Designer Steroids	Testosterone is the most common one.	Increased muscle mass and strength, cosmetic appearance of the body, and increased aggression.	Acne, heart problems, depression, and "roid rage." Females will gain male features including facial hair, deeper voice, abnormal menstrual cycles, and cessation of breast development.

Figure 16.1 Performance-Enhancing Drugs

1. Alcohol is often taken in larger amounts or over a longer period than was intended.

2. There is a persistent desire or unsuccessful efforts to cut down or control alcohol use.

3. A great deal of time is spent in activities necessary to obtain alcohol, use alcohol, or recover from its effects.

4. Craving, or a strong desire or urge to use alcohol.

5. Recurrent alcohol use resulting in a failure to fulfill major role obligations at work, school, or home.

6. Continued alcohol use despite having persistent or recurrent social or interpersonal problems caused or exacerbated by the effects of alcohol.

7. Important social, occupational, or recreational activities are given up or reduced because of alcohol use.

8. Recurrent alcohol use in situations in which it is physically hazardous.

9. Alcohol use is continued despite knowledge of having a persistent or recurrent physical or psychological problem that is likely to have been caused or exacerbated by alcohol.

10. Tolerance, as defined by either of the following:

a) A need for markedly increased amounts of alcohol to achieve intoxication or desired effect.

b) A markedly diminished effect with continued use of the same amount of alcohol.

11. Withdrawal, as manifested by either of the following:

a) The characteristic withdrawal syndrome for alcohol:

   A. Cessation of (or reduction in) alcohol use that has been heavy and prolonged.

   B. Two (or more) of the following, developing within several hours to a few days after Criterion A:

(1) autonomic hyperactivity (e.g. sweating or pulse rate greater than 100)

(2) increased hand tremor

(3) insomnia

(4) nausea or vomiting

(5) transient visual, tactile, or auditory hallucinations or illusions

(6) psychomotor agitation

(7) anxiety

(8) grand mal seizures

b) Alcohol is taken to relieve or avoid withdrawal symptoms.

Energy Drinks

This section targets the use of energy drinks to enhance performance. Energy drinks are not advised for use with exercise (Schumaker, 2014) due to their high levels of caffeine. The caffeine in energy drinks has a diuretic effect which causes the body to lose water, leading to dehydration. In addition, high levels of caffeine can lead to headaches, nervousness, increased heart rate and respirations, tremors and nausea. Research shows that energy drinks make the heart's palpitations stronger. Add into that the hard work your heart is already doing when you skate and it can be a recipe for disaster for those with underlying heart conditions. Though these negative effects are unlikely to turn up during moderate exercise with moderate amounts of caffeine (WebMD, 2014), we know roller derby is anything but moderate.

Energy drinks are not the same thing as sports drinks which are designed to rehydrate you and replenish your electrolytes. One is made for exertion and the other is not, but the way energy drink companies market their products, such as using extreme sports, it makes it very difficult to know the difference.

Caffeine is the most commonly used performance enhancing chemical among athletes so chances are you will choose to use it. If you do, it is best to be an informed consumer. Read labels so you can make informed decisions about what you are putting into your body. A regular cup of coffee has about 100 mg of caffeine. The maximum daily recommended amount of caffeine that a healthy adult should consume is 300–400 mg. Note this guideline does not take into consideration the added effects of intense activity levels. (The National Collegiate Athletic Association bans urine concentration levels of caffeine over 15 mcg/mL, which is about the equivalent of 8 regular cups of coffee.) Additionally, know the name of other sources of caffeine such as guayusa, yaupon, and guarana which may also be ingredients in energy drinks.

Banning Substance Use

Substance use in roller derby is not an easy black and white issue. Part of the complexity lies in the huge spectrum that substances fall on — from legal and socially acceptable ones like caffeine and supplements on one end to definitely illegal and socially unaccepted ones like methamphetamines on the other end. And then somewhere in the middle are substances that are legal but that skaters are not supposed to skate under the influence of, such as marijuana (legal in some states), alcohol, and performance-enhancing substances that vary in their legality.

Professional sports organizations and the International Roller Sports Federation (FIRS), which is recognized by the International Olympic Committee (IOC), have adopted the World Anti-Doping Agency's (WADA) "Code" banning performance-enhancing substances in categories such as Anabolic Steroids, Diuretics, Narcotics, Stimulants, Cannabinoids, Alcohol, Beta-Blockers, and Hormones. WFTDA and individual leagues ban skating while "impaired" and some leagues ban any illicit activities. However, our sport has not gotten to the point of doing any formal drug testing and most leagues don't have a stance on performance-enhancing substances. As food for thought, here are some pros and cons to allowing performance-enhancing substance use in sports (adapted from procon.org, 2014):

Personal freedom:

Pro: Athletes should have the right to weigh the potential health risks and benefits of performance-enhancing drugs and decide for themselves.

Con: When a situation becomes life threatening or negatively affects others, people lose the right to choose for themselves.

Unfair advantage:

Pro: Athletes do not gain an unfair advantage because access to performance-enhancing drugs is available to everyone.

Con: Athletes take performance-enhancing drugs to gain an advantage and those who use them will keep upping their intake to keep their advantage.

Drugs vs. Technology:

Pro: There is no difference between getting help with performance through advanced training and high tech equipment and taking drugs because both don't solely rely on an athlete's personal effort.

Con: The improvement in performance that can come from drug use far surpasses what can be gained from the most sophisticated and costly nonpharmaceutical interventions known to sports science.

Sportsmanship:

Pro: An athlete who takes an enhancing drug is no less courageous, dedicated and committed (words used in WADA's definition of "spirit of sport") than one who doesn't.

Con: Anti-doping programs seek to preserve the essence of sport which is the celebration of the human spirit, body and mind.

Athletes as role models:

Pro: The most reliable indicator of teen use of performance-enhancing drugs is their own self, esteem and body image.

Con: Young fans try to emulate much of what their favorite sports stars do. They will wear the same fashions, like the same brands, try to emulate their role models' training regimens and so will be influenced by their drug use.

Sports fans:

Pro: In major league sports such as baseball and football, drug use has not had an impact on audience interest.

Con: Fans will become bored as they begin to see games as less about skill and more about chemically induced brute strength and endurance.

Characteristics of Substance Abusers

- Change in behavior (being late to practice when they used to be on time, missing practice when they used to have great attendance, lack of motivation when they used to be very driven)

- Muscle twitches and tremors

- Poor hygiene and grooming

- Profuse sweating

- Major personality changes (going from social to isolated, patient to irritable)

- Impaired judgment

- Poor coordination

If you or someone on your team is suspected of having a substance problem, use the same intervention recommendations described earlier in the chapter for eating disorders.

SELF-HYPNOSIS

Throw out any ideas you might have about self-hypnosis having anything to do with making people do things against their will. The practice of self-hypnosis has nothing to do with those side shows at the fair where people end up walking around quacking like a duck. *Self-hypnosis* means that you are putting yourself into a hypnotic state.

Hypnosis is not:

- Mind control

- Brain washing

- Sleep

- Being unconscious

When under hypnosis a person is:

- Aware

- In control

- Able to come out of hypnosis whenever they want

- In a natural and harmless state

Being in a state of hypnosis means you are in a highly focused state where your suggestibility is heightened. Suggestions that you make to yourself while in this state become ingrained in your mind in a very deep and powerful way. Actions that you take in your day to day life will grow out of these suggestions and begin to make them reality. Self-hypnosis can help you to achieve your best performance when you make suggestions to yourself that represent your derby goals. Michael Cohen (2010–2011) describes the following steps for using self-hypnosis to realize your goals:

1. Sit in a comfortable chair with your legs and feet uncrossed.

2. Look up at the ceiling and take in a deep breath and close your eyes.

Pick a point on the ceiling and fix your gaze on that point. While you keep your eyes fixed on that point, take in a deep breath and hold it for as long as is comfortable. Then as you breathe out, repeat the suggestion, *My eyes are tired and heavy and I want to SLEEP NOW.* Repeat this process to yourself another couple of times and let your eyes close. It is important to tell yourself this as if you mean it, in a gentle but convincing manner.

3. Allow your body to become loose and limp like a rag doll.

Slowly, with intention, count down silently from five to zero. Tell yourself that with each and every count you're becoming more and more relaxed. Stay in this relaxed state for a few minutes while focusing on your breathing. Notice the rise and fall of your diaphragm and chest. Be aware of how relaxed your body is becoming without you even having to try to relax. The less you try, the more relaxed you become.

4. Picture an image that represents a situation you wish to master and see yourself achieving that goal.

Visualize your goal for 30 seconds. Chapter 9 describes how to make effective mental pictures.

5. Repeat your positive suggestion to yourself three times.

Rules for suggestions:

1. Say it as if you mean it. Friendly yet firm.

2. Suggestions need to be phrased positively and in the present tense. For example, say *I play well with everyone on my team* instead of *I won't fight with my teammates.*

3. Make suggestions specific and realistic. Review how to set great goals in Chapter 3 if needed.

4. Repeat suggestions. Advertisers know the value of suggestions, which is why they repeat commercials over and over again.

6. When ready come back to the room by counting up from one to five and opening your eyes.

Tell yourself that you are becoming aware of your surroundings and at the count of five you will open your eyes. Count up from one to five in a lively, energetic manner. At the count of five open your eyes.

Here is an example of how self-hypnosis could be used to help a jammer who has been having performance anxiety. This skater had a bad experience at a game a few months ago where she made a big mistake while jamming and there was a loud crowd reaction. She had been tired, was not focusing properly and had cut in front of several opposing skaters in a high pressure situation. Lately when she has been jamming the intensity of all eyes being on her has been getting to her and she has been freezing up. She has been so worried about making an error that she can barely play. She has a big game coming up and wants to be able to play like her old carefree self.

This skater would picture herself jamming in a game without holding back. A sample imagery script follows:

I picture myself approaching the pack with the other team's jammer far behind me. I know I have time to score all my points and call it off before she gets there. I am confident in my awareness of where all the skaters are: my teammates, the opposing blockers and the opposing jammer. I am faster than their blockers. I am untouchable. I can see the holes in their walls and I burst through them without hesitation. As soon as my hips are past their last blocker I call it off.

After visualizing this for 30 seconds she would make her suggestion three times, *I am a fearless jammer, I am a fearless jammer, I am a fearless jammer.*

Self-hypnosis, like the other mental toughness skills in this book, requires practice so keep at it and you'll be able to realize it's benefits.

17

EXCELLENCE IN COACHING

"I need somebody that A, pushes me and B, understands if I'm having an off day and to let it be. Just let me have my off day because I'll get back into it and I'll be fine."

— Punching Judy, age 47, skating 10 years

Up until now, all of the chapters in this book have been geared primarily towards the individual skater. This chapter is about how to be an excellent coach. It is also meant for the individual skater to read so you can be empowered with knowledge about the kind of coaching you deserve and should expect. Being involved in roller derby can have an important positive influence on a skater's self-esteem and character development. Whenever somebody talks about the positive aspects of roller derby, they always mention how it has built their self-confidence or improved their feelings of self-worth. Here are some ways that coaches can help to ensure that roller derby is a positive experience in a skater's life.

Coaches Expectations Can Become Reality

Coaches can knowingly or unknowingly influence a skater's performance which in turn influences the skater's self-confidence. Some coaches form expectations about a skater's potential ability. The coach may have high or low expectations of certain skaters. These expectations can be based on factors such as a skater's physical appearance, athletic experience or age. This can be a problem when the coach:

- spends more time at practice on "high expectation" athletes

- shows more warmth and positive emotions to high expectation athletes

- lowers expectations of what skills some athletes will learn, creating a lower standard of performance

- is less persistent in teaching difficult skills to "low expectation" athletes

- provides reinforcement and praise for high expectation athletes after a successful performance but gives less helpful feedback to low expectation athletes, such as praise after a mediocre performance

- gives high expectation athletes more instructional and informational feedback

Obviously, the skater who gets more positive and instructional feedback from coaches will show more improvement and enjoy the experience more. But what happens to those other skaters? Low expectation skaters will show poorer performances because they got less coaching time and less helpful reinforcement. Low expectation skaters will have lower self-confidence. Low expectation skaters will blame their failures on a lack of ability instead of lack of effort. This will support their ideas that they aren't any good and have little chance of getting better.

It is important for coaches to be aware of any biases they might have so they can guard against treating skaters differently. If they can be aware of how their own attitudes and actions help produce these results they can avoid creating a negative self-fulfilling prophecy.

"I think who leads a team is really important. I've seen a lot of teams and their coaches and they kind of mirror each other."

— Wombpunch, age 26, skating 4 years

Coaches Must Create A Positive Learning Environment

The way that coaches handle their skaters' mistakes may be the single most crucial thing that they do. Fear of making mistakes can limit a skater's performance because the skater will hold back and not give 100%. Coaches must make skaters believe that making mistakes is okay and a necessary part of the learning process.

Coaches can have skaters come up with a physical ritual to use to get past a mistake so they can focus on the next play. For example, skaters can pretend to dust off their uniform to "brush it off" or make a fist and then open it to "let it go". Rituals remind skaters that mistakes are going to happen and the most important thing is how they react right after a mistake.

Sometimes a skater's fear of mistakes comes from an over-emphasis on winning. Too much focus on winning increases a skater's anxiety. Too much anxiety decreases self-confidence, negatively affects performance, and takes away the FUN.

> *Research shows that athletes who perceive their coaches as having a democratic approach to decision making have lower levels of burnout (Harris, 2005).*

Focusing on being competitive for upcoming games is great for keeping skaters working hard and motivated at practice, but come game day the team should have other goals in to addition winning. This can be anything from not letting the other team get in your head to keeping your game faces on the whole time to executing a certain play. This way a team and skaters can feel like winners regardless of the scoreboard.

Coaches must emphasize the constant learning process by turning every game into a positive learning experience by drawing out lessons that can be applied to the next game. Coaches shouldn't allow skaters to dwell on losses or gloat over wins. Coaches should have the team begin preparing for the next game at the very next practice.

Coaches Can Help Skaters To Maximize Motivation

Sometimes an athlete feels that they are going to fail no matter what and there is nothing they can do about it. This is called *learned helplessness*. Learned helplessness can develop in athletes who have come to believe that their actions have no effect on what they are attempting to accomplish. Failure is attributed to lack of abilities and success is attributed to reasons such as luck. This could be the skater who doesn't like trying new skills and always starts in the back of the line. Or the skater who gravitates towards extreme competitive situations, like racing against the fastest or slowest skater on the team. Success or failure is almost certain in these situations.

Coaches can help a skater overcome learned helplessness. When a skater successfully executes a skill at practice the coach should:

- Tell them it was because of their awesome effort.

- Tell them it was because of their ability.

- Don't tell them it was due to luck.

- Don't tell them it was because the task was easy.

- Don't give insincere or false feedback.

Coaches Must Give Helpful Criticism

Feedback from coaches should be genuine and specific. Coaches should not say "Good job!" when the skater knew it wasn't. Give skaters encouragement combined with technical information on how to correct their mistakes. Instead of saying "Focus!" say "Look at the jammer". Instead of saying "Relax!" say "Loosen your shoulders."

Coaches can use a positive "sandwich" method when correcting errors. The sandwich method cushions the correction, or the "meat" of the message, between two positive messages. For example, "You had great enthusiasm and couldn't wait to get going. Next time wait for the whistle so you don't get a false start penalty. You'll get it!"

"You've been timing your hits really well"

"Make sure you're focusing on their jammer and not getting distracted"

"You're getting to be a huge threat!"

Skaters should be rewarded for correct technique regardless of the outcome. If they do everything right but miss the block, give them positive reinforcement. Making a hit when the form is incorrect is not helpful in the long run. Coaches should demand effort, not results.

Coaches can try using the 5:1 Magic Ratio, recommended by the Liberty Mutual Positive Play Program, of five praises to one criticism. This ensures that the skater's *emotional tanks* are being filled. If a coach tries to catch a skater doing things right, rather than looking for errors, this becomes easier to do. Many coaches make the mistake of only providing encouragement, attention or instruction to an athlete when they do something wrong.

The following describes an incident involving a coach yelling at an athlete for making a mistake and the long-lasting negative repercussions. "The coach's comments were so demeaning and degrading, her tone of voice so penetrating and hurtful, her non-verbal body language so piercing that the athlete shut down and tuned out anything positive that was said thereafter. The whole situation was unfortunate because the athlete, talented yet low in self-confidence, began to fear failure, was scared to make a mistake, and never quite recovered for the rest of the season (Williams, 2006, p. 176)."

"I don't like the screaming and the aggressiveness and the belittling." — *EMTease, age 33, skating 5 years*

Great Coaches Have Great Qualities.

Skaters need a coach that is open, honest, genuine, passionate, fair, consistent and understanding. A great coach must be able to gain the respect and trust of his or her skaters. There is a fine line that great coaches are able to walk between maintaining authority and being approachable. Skaters need to feel that their coach has credibility, that their coach sees their contributions as valuable and that they are being treated with dignity. Superb communication skills are crucial for excellent coaching!

One research study on gymnasts listed the behaviors those athletes wanted the most in a coach (Massimo, 1973):

Use minimal verbiage. Coaches should avoid overteaching. When working on improving a skill a coach should only pick one thing for the skater to correct rather than a whole list of things. The coach can briefly tell the skater what to adjust, perhaps with a physical demonstration, but then have the skater put it into practice.

Have a sense of humor. This means being able to laugh at yourself and with others, not at another. Sarcasm is not an appropriate form of humor for coaching.

Use individual psychology. Coaches should address the needs of skaters as individuals. Some skaters need a lot of attention and others can practically coach themselves.

---

3 Levels Of Listening

Research has identified three levels of listening (Rosenfeld and Wilder, 1990):

Active listening is when the listener is concerned with the content, intent, and feelings the speaker is trying to convey. This is the most ideal form of listening.

Inattentive listening is then the listener tunes out once they think they have enough information to figure out what the speaker is trying to say. The listener may understand the meaning of the message being transmitted but may miss out on important emotional content or underlying ideas.

Arrogant listeners are only interested in what they have to say. They wait for breaks in the conversation so they can hear themselves talk.

Have technical competency. A person can be a great coach and not the best performer. A person can also be a great athlete and not have the personal skills or technical knowledge to be a great coach.

Appreciate the sociology of the team. Coaches should not only be able to deal with individuals but also how those skaters work together. Coaches should be able to effectively end small interpersonal conflicts before they escalate but should also be able to ignore minor issues that will shortly blow over.

A derby skater's experience in the sport can have lifelong effects on their psychological development. A coach plays a huge part in ensuring skaters have a positive, fulfilling derby experience and gain lessons that can enrich them for the rest of their lives.

"The worst thing in my mind would be making me feel bad for being a weaker skater."

–Paisley, age 21, fresh meat

18

CONCLUSION

"Derby as a sport has seen me through death, failed relationships, a degree in science, and births. My derby sisters have been there to deep me sane, help me smile, and know that everything will be ok. Derby has shaped me into a better version of myself." — Loogie Vuitton, age 32, skating 6 years

Now that you have read the Mental Toughness Guide: Roller Derby, you have knowledge about the abilities you need to be able to play at your absolute best. Mental toughness skills, like physical skills, must be practiced. It is not enough to just read this book once and put it aside. Pick a few skills to work on mastering and then go back for more to add to your tool box.

As your derby career evolves so will your need for mental toughness skills. As a new skater, you may just want to have the courage to be able to try new things at practice in front of the veterans. As a more advanced skater, you may be more interested in how to capitalize on the benefits of imagery to be able to overcome a mental barrier. This book will evolve with you as you will be able to understand the lessons on a deeper and deeper level every time you read it.

Let's Review!

Let's review some of the key concepts from each of the chapters in the Mental Toughness Guide: Roller Derby:

Chapter 1: What Is Mental Toughness Training?

- Mental toughness training uses concepts from psychology to help athletes perform at their very best.

- Core mental toughness skills include negative thought stopping, energy management, focus, goal setting, motivation and confidence.

- Experts say an athlete's performance is at least 60% psychological.

- Mental toughness skills, like physical skating skills, need to be practiced!

Chapter 1: Be Self-Aware

- An aspect of being mindful is being aware, but not judgmental, of your emotions.

- Flow state or the zone is a state of complete absorption, where time disappears and your performance is effortless.

- Being present means you aren't time traveling to the future or stuck in the past. You are fully here. *Now.*

- The phrase, *This is it*, can remind you to appreciate and savor derby moments.

- Self-awareness demands honesty.

Chapter 3: Set Goals

- Set goals that are **s**pecific, **m**easurable, **a**ction-oriented, **r**ealistic, and **t**imely. Be sure to **e**valuate and **re**-evaluate goals often!

- Will power is involved in achieving goals.

- Be sure to set short term and long term goals, practice and game goals.

- Establish pre-game routines to focus you in the right direction and on the right things.

- Research the game venue to cut down on competition jitters and increase confidence.

Chapter 4: Focus On Your Focus

- There are three elements of focus. Selective attention is the ability to focus on the most appropriate thing. Concentration means being able to sustain your attention over time. Attentional control is the ability to shift between the different dimensions of attention to meet the changing demands of the game.

- The dimensions of attention are broad, narrow, internal and external. When we are assessing we are using a broad-external focus. When we are analyzing we are using a broad-internal focus. When we mentally rehearse what we are going to do we are using a narrow-internal focus. When we are focused on performing the immediate task we are using a narrow-external focus.

- Our focus can be thought of as a flashlight beam. There are three focusing errors: 1) Having your flashlight beam too broad and focusing on too many things at once; 2) Pointing your flashlight beam in the wrong direction and having it focused on the wrong thing; 3) Having your flashlight beam too narrow so that it doesn't shine on enough things or not shifting it from one thing to another rapidly enough.

- Stress narrows our focus by limiting our field of awareness. We want this to a certain degree but if our focus becomes too restricted we will miss important elements.

Chapter 5: Defeat Distractions

- Successful athletes are able to adapt, refocus and stay positive in the face of distractions.

- Choking happens when an athlete becomes too conscious of processes that should be performed automatically. A simple solution is to get out of your head by focusing intently on something mundane in your environment.

- Don't waste your focus thinking about things that are outside of your control. We can only control our own thoughts and actions.

- Mistakes can be a source of distraction when athletes can't leave them in the past or are worried about making them in the future. Use refocusing techniques such as *Park It* to be able to get your concentration back to the present moment.

Chapter 6: Manage Your Energy

- An athlete who can manage her energy is able to bring her arousal levels up or down as needed.

- The stress-performance relationship can be demonstrated by an inverted-U. The higher our stress levels, the better our performance, but only to a point and then too much stress inhibits our performance.

- The flight or fight response does all kinds of crazy things to our physiology such as giving us tense muscles, sweaty skin, slowed digestion, widened pupils and butterflies in our stomach. Learn to interpret pre-game nerves as signs of readiness to play! If you are too keyed up, use relaxation techniques to bring energy levels down.

- Pacing involves knowing how much energy is required of you for a game and being able to make sure you can keep your energy consistently high the entire time.

Chapter 7: Think Positively

- Our thoughts influence our feelings which lead to us to act in certain ways. By recognizing, challenging and changing negative or unhelpful thinking patterns we can change the outcome to one that is in line with where we want to be in derby and in life.

- Red flag words like *should, must, never, hate, have to,* and *always* are limiting. Change them to words like *could, might, sometimes, it would be nice if,* and *there's a chance of* in order to expand possibilities.

- Faulty, automatic thinking styles such as all-or-nothing, catastrophizing, overgeneralizing and minimization can get in the way of our success.

- Challenge faulty beliefs by asking questions such as, "What is the worst thing that could happen?," "What is the evidence?," and "Is there another way of looking at things?"

Chapter 8: Create Confidence

- Confidence comes from things like past accomplishments, seeing others perform well, having trust in your coaches' and teammates' abilities and decisions and feeling good about your body. The biggest source of self-confidence is past accomplishments.

- Lack of confidence comes from places like fear of failure, fear of success and fear of injury. Some self-doubt is helpful because it prevents contentment and keeps you trying.

- There are three types of confidence. Overconfidence occurs when one thinks their skills are greater than they actually are. Lack of confidence happens when you have the skills but aren't able to perform them under pressure when it counts. Optimal self-confidence is when your confidence matches your skills and abilities.

- A self-fulfilling prophecy is when you cause something to happen by expecting it to happen. Avoid creating a negative self-fulfilling prophecy by expecting to be successful in your endeavors.

- Our thoughts, feelings and actions are all interrelated. Thinking confidently will lead to confident actions. Acting confident can lead to feeling confident. Feeling confident will lead to believing you can do it.

- Use affirmations to boost confidence. An affirmation is a short, simple, positive phrase stated in the present tense such as, *I am a powerhouse.*

Chapter 9: Use Imagery

- Imagery, visualization or mental practice is the process of vividly picturing ourselves performing skills or dealing with certain situations. Our brains can't distinguish between actual and imaginary events so it will build the same brain-body connections as if you were actually going through the motions in real life.

- You can image from two different perspectives: internal and external.

- Good images are as realistic as possible and incorporate as many of your senses as possible: smell, touch, taste, sound and sight. Skaters should also involve their desired thoughts and feelings in their images.

- Two aspects of solid imagery are vividness and controllability. Vividness has to do with how detailed an image is. Controllability refers to the ability to manipulate an image.

Chapter 10: Win With Grace, Lose With Class

- Wins and losses are not absolute values. If your team gives it everything it's got but loses to a better team that loss may not mean as much as losing because of careless errors or a breakdown in communication. Conversely, beating a team that is clearly at a lower skill level than your team should not feel as significant as beating a team as the underdogs.

- Teams should be sure to focus on performance and process goals along with outcome goals. Performance and process goals are things you have control over and are independent of the score. Outcome goals focus on the end results of competition — usually winning.

- There can be a lot of pressure in being one of the top skaters on a team. These pressures can come from both internal sources such as worries about letting the team down and external sources like coaches and teammates telling you, "We're depending on you."

- It can be challenging to play your best during game situations where your team is drastically up or down in score.

- Be sure to use positive attributions such as taking credit for your hard work or holding poor processes responsible following a win or loss. Avoid negative attributions for a loss such as taking all the blame or blaming others.

- Having a healthy competitive attitude means seeking out opponents of equal skill level, being able to perform well when being evaluated, trying harder in the face of failure, being motivated by success and putting a lot of effort into achieving derby goals.

- How you handle a loss or disappointment defines you as a person. Learn to accept losing or setbacks as a necessary and helpful part of the realization or your dreams.

Chapter 11: Get Back In The Game After An Injury

- A skater may feel guilt, hopelessness, anger, identity loss, loneliness, frustration and lack of confidence following an injury. How a skater perceives or interprets their injury will determine how they respond to it.

- Coaches must allow skaters to go through an emotional recovery process as well as a physical recovery process. Just because a skater has been medically cleared does not mean they are psychologically ready to return.

- Teammates can help an injured skater by including them in social activities and practice activities.

- Skaters with a history of stressors, certain personality characteristics and lack of coping resources puts them at a higher risk for injury.

- Skaters can come back to practice confident and stress free by using strategies like going to practice as often as possible while injured, using a peer mentor, learning to separate pain from injury and allowing themselves the appropriate and healthy expression of emotions.

Chapter 12: Be A Good Sport

- Good sportsmanship involves believing there is a right and a wrong way to act in sports and striving to act the right way — sports morality!

- Teams can help their skaters with sportsmanship by breaking down general codes of conduct into specific actions and behaviors.

- Levels of Moral Reasoning is a model that sports psychologists use to show how an athlete will develop from a perspective that is self-centered to one that is concerned with what is in the best interest for all involved.

- Aggressive behavior refers to actions with an *intent* to harm or injure a person.

- Cocky, arrogant, egotistical or entitled behavior can destroy team harmony and ultimately set a skater up for failure.

- Social skills, independence and hope are traits that will help you to deal with disappointment.

- Turn negative feelings of jealousy into positive feelings of inspiration.

- Mean girls detract from everyone's best game whether you *are* the mean girl or are suffering from the actions of a mean girl.

- Improve sportsmanship by practicing the Six Pillars of Character developed by the Josephson Institute: Trustworthiness, Respect, Responsibility, Fairness, Caring and Citizenship.

Chapter 13: Team Building

- A team is a group of people that work together to accomplish a common goal. A team is more than the sum of its parts.

- The Ringelmann Effect demonstrates the phenomenon that the more people there are involved in a task, the less amount of work each person puts in.

- Clear definition and acceptance of roles on a team helps avoid misunderstanding and resentment.

- Cliques and problems with leadership are some issues that teams can have.

- Be aware of non-verbal communication including lack of eye contact and eye rolling. Make sure you are giving the message you want to give.

- Ways to minimize problems with drama consist of avoiding gossip, speaking up when you have concerns, respecting leadership, tolerating and appreciating and being humble.

- Learn how to increase your chances of successfully resolving conflicts. Conflict resolution skills involve using I Messages, sticking to one problem at a time, knowing how to cool off, being able to apologize and knowing how to let things go.

Chapter 14: Prevent Burnout

- Burnout is defined as "a physical, emotional, and social withdrawal from a formerly enjoyable sport activity (Weinberg & Gould, 2011, p. 496)."

- Some of the signs and symptoms of burnout are physical fatigue, chronic injuries, loss of fun, loss of meaning and difficulty focusing.

- The three main characteristics of burnout are measured by the MBI: emotional exhaustion, depersonalization and a low sense of personal accomplishment.

- The Cognitive-Affective Stress Model explains burnout as occurring when the skater has more demands placed on them than they have the resources to handle — over time they will become stressed.

- Some of the causes of burnout are training at a young age, year round training, coaching style, repetitive drills, deteriorating performance, losing streaks, pressures to win and social problems.

- Individuals who are perfectionistic, competitive, self-critical, have a fear of failure, have low self-esteem and are anxious are more prone to burnout.

- Burnout can be prevented by doing things like learning to cope with stress, keeping training exciting and fun, taking breaks, focusing on short term goals, taking recovery seriously, reframing unhelpful thinking patterns and staying physically healthy.

- One way to manage stress is by using the Four A's (Smith et al., 2014). **Avoid** stress whenever possible. Try to **alter** a stressful situation that can't be avoided. If the situation can't be avoided or altered, then try to **adapt** yourself to be able to deal with it better. Finally, find **acceptance** of yourself, others and the situation.

- Signs of stress include dizziness, memory problems, poor judgment, racing thoughts, moodiness, aches and pains, grinding teeth and muscle tension.

- We can create resilience in the face of adversity by uncovering the faulty beliefs that are leading us to feel negative emotions. Use the ABC model where A= the adversity, B= our beliefs about why the situation happened and C= the emotional or behavioral consequence for the belief. By changing our beliefs we can create more positive responses to adversity.

Chapter 15: Life After Derby

- Reasons for retiring from derby include work, school, finances, decreased performance, age, injury and deselection.

- Skaters who mourn the loss of derby may go through some or all of the five stages of grief: denial, anger, sadness, bargaining and acceptance.

- You can smooth the transition out of competitive derby by planning for retirement *before* you retire. Decide what role derby will play in your life, respect the other parts of your life while you are still competing and make plans to continue exercising!

Chapter 16: More Mental Toughness Stuff

- Signs and symptoms of eating disorders include hoarding food, difficulty handling days off from exercise, decreased body temperature/sensitivity to cold, disappearing after meals, slowed heart rate and blood pressure and ritualistic eating.

- Having performance anxiety, perfectionism, history of trauma and being involved in endurance sports or sports where appearances are important put an athlete at higher risk for developing an eating disorder.

- Help to prevent eating disorders for you and your team by doing things like discouraging dieting, learning about eating to maximize performance, banishing comments about size/shape from practice, being aware of self-consciousness that might result from uniform issues, finding the right balance between weight and performance, knowing eating habits can be contagious and focusing on fitness over body weight.

- Psyching out your opponent means psychologically getting them into a position where you can dominate them physically. Methods include trash talking, being a mystery, playing it cool and making them angry.

> *Roller derby can give skaters a sense of identity, self-confidence, and a purpose.*

- Athletes may use substances for physical, social or psychological reasons.

- Substances fall into two categories: recreational drugs and performance-enhancing drugs. Recreational drugs include cocaine, methamphetamines and marijuana. Performance-enhancing drugs include hGH, diuretics, beta-blockers and anabolic steroids.

- Substance problems can be diagnosed on a spectrum from mild to moderate to severe.

- Energy drinks are not advised for use with exercise due to the high levels of caffeine.

- The topic of legalization vs. prohibition of substances is a complex and controversial one with proponents on both sides of the fence.

- Characteristics of substance users include muscle twitches or tremors, profuse sweating, poor coordination, major personality changes and poor hygiene.

- Self-hypnosis is not mind control, brain washing, sleep or being unconscious. When under self-hypnosis a person is aware, in control, in a natural and harmless state and able to come out of it whenever they want.

- You can use self-hypnosis to achieve your derby goals by making suggestions to yourself while being in a state of heightened suggestibility.

Chapter 17: Excellence In Coaching

- Coaches need to be aware of their expectations regarding an athlete's potential ability. Having low expectations of a skater can lead to a negative self-fulfilling prophecy.

- Coaches can prevent learned helplessness by helping a skater to feel their efforts play a part in their success.

- Coaches should give feedback that is both genuine and specific.

- Coaches can cushion corrections between two positive messages using a "sandwich" method.

- Coaches should include encouragement, attention and instruction when skaters are doing things correctly, not only when they are doing things wrong.

- Great coaches use minimal verbiage, have a sense of humor, use individual psychology, have technical competence and appreciate the sociology of the team.

Fulfilling Your Potential

Abraham Maslow (1908–1970), an American psychologist, created a theory of psychological health based on fulfilling innate needs in priority. It is a theory that focuses on how we fulfill our potential. The five-stage model includes Physiological needs, Safety needs, Social needs, Self-Esteem needs and, at the top, Self-Actualization needs. One must meet the basic needs first or progress can't be made. According to Maslow, motivation to fulfill these needs is not based on external rewards, but based on an innate motivation.

Maslow's theory can be modified to illustrate one's journey to mental toughness along your roller derby career. It is important to note the pinnacle, Self-Actualization, is a direction, not a destination. It is like journeying west. One never actually arrives at west and one never is done self-actualizing.

"There are no perfect human beings"

– Abraham Maslow

Physiological needs: These include basic needs such as finding a league, getting fit, getting enough sleep, dedicating yourself to derby, setting your first derby goals, getting a derby name and being physically and emotionally healthy.

Safety needs: Finding freedom from fear, getting gear savvy, surviving your first game, learning how your league is run and understanding the rules of the sport.

Social needs: Developing a greater understanding of game strategy, being able to see the big picture during games, being able to get along with teammates, realizing the derby sisterhood, finding your place in the league, playing to your teammates' strengths and balancing derby and personal life.

Self-Esteem needs: Having gratitude for mind and body, awareness and honesty about skill level, getting status as a derby girl, having self-respect and respect from others, achieving derby goals and having confidence in coaches, training and skills.

Self-Actualization: This includes seeking personal growth and challenging experiences, doing what is best for the team rather than for one's self, realizing personal potential and self-fulfillment.

Figure 18.1 Maslow's Hierarchy of Needs

15 Characteristics Of Self-Actualizers

1. They perceive reality efficiently and can tolerate uncertainty.

2. They accept themselves and others for what they are.

3. They are spontaneous in thought and action.

4. They are problem-centered, not self-centered.

5. They have an unusual sense of humor.

6. They are able to look at life objectively.

7. They are highly creative.

8. They are resistant to enculturation, but not purposely unconventional.

9. They are concerned for the welfare of humanity.

10. They are capable of deep appreciation of basic life experiences.

11. They establish deeply satisfying interpersonal relationships with a few people.

12. They have peak experiences (especially joyous moments in life).

13. They have a need for privacy.

14. They have democratic attitudes.

15. They have strong moral/ethical standards.

Make sure FUN is a fundamental part of your derby experience!

Behaviors That Can Help Lead A Person To Self-Actualization

- Experiencing life like a child, with full absorption and concentration
- Trying new things instead of sticking to safe paths
- Listening to your own feelings in evaluating experiences instead of the voice of tradition, authority or the majority
- Avoiding game playing and being honest
- Taking responsibility and working hard
- Trying to identify your defenses and having the courage to give them up

Try this: Are You Mentally Tough?

Retake the quiz that you took at the beginning of this book:

1. Before a game I
   a. Always set goals
   b. Sometimes set goals
   c. Never set goals

2. Whether I am winning or losing I
   a. Always believe in myself
   b. Believe in myself only when I'm winning
   c. Rarely believe in myself and think I'm a failure

3. Distractions during a game
   a. Don't bother me
   b. Sometimes bother me, but I can easily refocus
   c. Take my focus fully away from my performance

4. My emotions, thoughts and breathing in a game are usually
   a. Something I can control and use to my advantage
   b. Inconsistent, but are in my control when I am doing well
   c. Not in my control, my breathing is too fast and I have a hard time reacting

5. After a game, the self-evaluation of my performance is
  a. Normally accurate about what my strengths and weaknesses were that day
  b Not always accurate, but I can pick out some key things I need to improve
  c. Never accurate because I don't ever evaluate my performance

---

Answers

A's are worth 3 points each. B's are worth 2 points each. C's are worth 0 points each.

12–15: You are very mentally tough.

8–11: You are somewhat mentally tough.

4–7: You could benefit from more mental toughness.

0–3: Uh oh, you need to learn some mental toughness skills.

Hopefully, your scores have improved as you've started to apply mental toughness skills to your derby game. Being a badass roller derby skater requires two things: physical skills and resolution. This book will help you to achieve the attitude of mind — the mental toughness — which will allow you to use your physical skills to be able to play at your absolute best. If you can also become a better person along the way then it is a win for everybody!

REFERENCES

American Psychiatric Association (2013). *Diagnostic and Statistical Manual of Mental Disorders* (5th Ed.). Arlington, VA: American Psychiatric Publishing.

Baron, R. A., & Richardson, D. R. (1994). *Human Aggression (Perspectives in Social Psychology)* (2nd Ed.). New York, NY: Plenum Press.

Berg, F. M. (1999). *Women Afraid to Eat: Breaking free in today's weight-obsessed world.* Hettinger, ND: Healthy Weight Publishing Network.

Brain Works Project (2014). *Coping Skills for Kids.* Retrieved from www.copingskills4kids.net

Caffeineinformer (2014). Retrieved from http://www.caffeineinformer.com

Cohen, M. (2010). *How to Use Self-Hypnosis to Achieve Your Goals.* Retrieved from www.hypnosisandhealing.co.uk

D. Stroir, B. (2012, August 17). Jealousy vs. Inspiration [Web log post]. Retrieved from www.bonniedstroir.blogspot.com

Dartmouth College (2014). *Guide 3: Understanding Our Response to Stress and Adversity.* Retrieved August 28, 2014, from www.dartmouth.edu

Etnier, J. L. (2009). *Bring Your 'A' Game.* Chapel Hill, NC: The University of North Carolina Press.

Farmer, S. (2012, March 21). *NFL hits Saints with severe sanctions for bounty program*. Retrieved from www.articles.latimes.com

Goldberg, A. (2014). *Burnout*. Retrieved August 26, 2014, from www.competitiveedge.com

Gould, D., Tuffey, S., Udry, E., & Loehr, J. (1996b). Burnout in competitive junior tennis players: II. A qualitative content analysis and case studies. *The Sport Psychologist, 10,* 341–366.

The Guardian (2009, May 4). *Serena Williams dismisses Safina's claim to top ranking*. Retrieved from www.theguardian.com

Guskiewicz, K. M., Marshall, S. W., McCrea, M., Cantu, R. C., Randolph, C., & Jordan, B. D. (2005). Association between recurrent concussion and late-life cognitive impairment in retired professional football players. *Neurosurgery, 57*(4), 719–726.

Guskiewjcz, K. M., Marshall, S. W., Bailes, J., McCrea, M., Harding, Jr., H. P., Mihalik, J. R., & Cantu, R. C. (2006). Recurrent Concussion and Risk of Depression in Retired Professional Football Players. *Medicine & Science in Sports & Exercise, 39*(6), 903–909.

Halverson, N. (2014, January 27). *Trash Talkers: Do they psyche out opponents?* Retrieved from www.news.discovery.com

Harris, B. S. (2005). *Coach and Athlete Burnout: the Role of Coaches' Decision-Making Style* (Master's thesis).

Josephson Institute (2014). *The T.E.A.M. Approach to Sportsmanship.* Retrieved from www.josephsoninstitute.org

Kabat-Zin, J. (1994). *Wherever You Go There You Are.* New York, NY: Hyperion.

Klein, J. Z., & Belson, K. (2014, April 10). *N.H.L. Promoted Violence Regardless of Health Risk, Players' Suit Says.* Retrieved from www.nytimes.com

Kliethernes, M. (2009). *The "What are you thinking?" Team.*

Liberty Mutual (2014). *Play Positive.* Retrieved August 23, 2014, from www.play-positive.libertymutual.com

Lynch, J. (2001). *Creative Coaching.* Champaign, IL: Human Kinetics.

Massimo, J. (1973). *A psychologist's approach to sport.* Paper presented at the New England Gymnastic Clinic. Newton, MA.

Matsumoto, N., Ackerman, K., Kurilla, A., Herrin, M., Anderson, C., Dupcak, S., & Post, W. (2014). *National Eating Disorders Association Toolkit for Coaches and Trainers.* . Retrieved September 20, 2014, from www.nationaleatingdisorders.org

Maximum Fitness (2006, January/February). *Head Games: How to Psych Out Your Opponent.* Retrieved from www.innerwarrior.com

Mayo Clinic Staff (2014). *Performance-enhancing drugs: Know the risks.* Retrieved from www.mayoclinic.org

Men's Health (2014). *Psych Out: Psych out enemies of all kinds with these confidence tricks.* Retrieved from www.innerwarrior.com

Mind Tools (2014). *The Wheel of Life: Finding Balance in Your Life.* Retrieved August 28, 2014, from

http://www.mindtools.com/pages/article/newHTE_93.htm

Orlick, T. (2008). *In Pursuit of Excellence* (4th Ed.). Champaign, IL: Human Kinetics.

Oxford (2014). *Oxford Dictionaries.* Retrieved from

www.oxforddictionaries.com

ProCon.org (2014). *Drug Use in Sports: Pros and Cons.* Retrieved from

http://sportsanddrugs.procon.org

Raedeke, T. D., & Smith, A. L. (2001). Development and preliminary validation of an athlete burnout measure. *Journal of Sport and Exercise Psychology, 23,* 281–306.

Rainey, D. W. (2008). *Trash Talk Experience of College Athletes.* Retrieved from http://webmedia.jcu.edu

Reivich, K., & Shatte', A. (2003). *The Resilience Factor: 7 Keys to Finding Your Inner Strength and Overcoming Life's Hurdles.* New York, NY: Broadway Books.

Rosenfeld, L., & Wilder, L. (1990). Communication fundamentals: Active listening. *Sport Psychology Training Bulletin, 1*(5), 1–8.

Schumaker, E. (2014, June 23). *Just How Dangerous Are Energy Drinks, Anyway?* Retrieved from www.huffingtonpost.com

Simmons, R. (2002). *Odd Girl Out.* New York, NY: Houghton Mifflin Harcourt Publishing Company.

Smith, M., Segal, R., & Segal, J. (2014, July). *Stress Symptoms, Signs and Causes.* Retrieved August 27, 2014, from www.helpguide.org

Solotaroff, P. (2014, August). *Confessions of an NFL Hitman.* Retrieved from www.mensjournal.com

Sportspsych (2014). *Sportspsych.* Retrieved August 28, 2014, from www.sportspsych.wikispaces.com

Tucker, A. (2012, July). *The Science of Choking Under Pressure.* Retrieved from www.smithsonianmag.com

University of Chicago (2014). *Five Finger Relaxation Technique.* Retrieved August 28, 2014, from www.counselinguchicago.edu

USA Rollersports (2014). *Code of Conduct.* Retrieved from www.teamusa.org

WebMD (2014). *Caffeine.* Retrieved from www.webmd.com

Weinberg, R. S., & Gould, D. (2011). *Foundations of Sport and Exercise Psychology* (5th ed.). Champaign, IL: Human Kinetics.

WFTDA (2014). *Code of Conduct.* Retrieved from www.wftda.com

Yesalis, C. E., & Bahrke, M. S. (2014). *Anabolic Steroids.* Retrieved from www.acsm.org

Williams, J. M. (2006). *Applied Sport Psychology* (5th ed.). New York, NY: McGraw Hill Higher Education.

ABOUT THE AUTHOR

Naomi "Sweetart" Weitz has been skating and coaching since May of 2006. She has a Master's degree in Psychology, is a practicing Licensed Mental Health Counselor, and is certified in Sports and Fitness Psychology. She is the founder and head coach of Spokannibals Roller Derby and Tournament Director for Spokarnage: A Killer Roller Derby Tournament. Naomi lives and skates in Spokane, WA.

ABOUT THE COVER DESIGNER & ARTIST

Skyler Weitz is a senior in high school and is studying graphic design. He was the first male, junior roller derby skater in the Inland Northwest, skating on a co-ed team under the name of Weeble #8bit. Skyler continues to break down barriers with his visual art. Skyler lives and goes to school in Spokane, WA.

Printed in Great Britain
by Amazon